SNOW CAMP
LOOKOUT

Enjoy

David Calahan

SNOW CAMP LOOKOUT

VIEW WITH A ROOM
Mouse Included

David Calahan

Illustrated by Barbara Kostal

IN-FORMS PUBLISHING
MEDFORD, OREGON
• 1 9 9 6 •

© 1996 by David Calahan

David Calahan
P.O. Box 1394
Jacksonville, Oregon 97530
USA

Published by
In-Forms Publishing
P.O. Box 8503
Medford, Oregon 97504

ISBN 0-9619808-1-8

FIRST EDITION

LIBRARY OF CONGRESS CATALOG CARD NUMBER: 96-76155.

Cover design by Barbara Kostal
Photos by author unless otherwise noted.
Snowflakes on cover and throughout the book
are designs from photographs in
Snow Crystals by W.A. Bentley and W.J. Humphreys,
Dover Publishing Inc., NY, NY.

Printed in the United States of America.

DEDICATION

To all the people who brought
Snow Camp Lookout back to life,
to those who wrote in the journal, and
to Barbara, who inspired me to create this book.

TABLE OF CONTENTS

continued

Table of Contents –
continued

Preface

When Snow Camp Lookout was restored and first opened to the public in June 1990, a journal was made available for all the visitors to write in. On my first visit to Snow Camp on September 23, 1993, I discovered the journal, read every entry and added my own. It was like a good novel, difficult to put down…giving a real glimpse into people's lives. Therein lies the basis for this book.

In writing *Snow Camp Lookout*, I wanted to maintain the style and flow of each individual "author's" comments. Sometimes I made slight alterations to the punctuation, structure or words in order to retain, for the reader, the essence of the writer's thoughts . There is much more material in the original journal than is found in the following pages. There were so many entries about the beauty, charm, view, clarity of the stars, movement of the fog, relentless wind, colors, privacy (usually), sunrises and sunsets, that I had to omit many of the duplicate comments.

It is also notable that many visitors are "repeats," coming back year after year. I'm sure this book will have mixed reviews from the regulars, since the more people who know about this wonderful place, the more difficult it will be to get the particular days you want to reserve. I can foresee a time when it may come to a computer raffle, such as those programs used to obtain trips down the popular rivers during the busy summer months.

Probably the most common phrase I read in the journal was, "We'll be back." Once you've had the opportunity to experience time in a glass house on "top of the world," it becomes addicting. Not everyone can spend time in a lookout, but this book can take you there through the entries of others in the Snow Camp journal.

Meet "Timothy," the mouse, who provides occasional entertainment. Feel the power of the wind at 4,223 feet. See the movement of the clouds in the sky and at times be part of the clouds as they swirl around you. Visualize the vivid colors. People on vacation must be truly moved to awaken early just to watch a simple sunrise. Perhaps you too will become a "lookout junkie" by either visiting one or vicariously through this book.

Enjoy!

Introduction

Snow Camp Lookout sits on a mountain top at 4,223 feet above sea level in the Coastal Mountain Range of southwest Oregon. The lookout is a 15' x 15' building with windows on all four sides (111 panes total). When Snow Camp Mountain was first used as a lookout site during World War I, the structure probably consisted of no more than a tent. No permanent building was constructed on the site until 1924, although fire-locating instruments were first used there in 1918. Lookout personnel lived at the ranger station down in Snow Camp Meadow and made the hike to the mountaintop each day to watch for fires. During World War II, Snow Camp was used as a place to watch for enemy aircraft, as were other lookouts along the west coast.

In 1958 the original structure was removed and the present building was erected and staffed each summer until 1972. It was renovated and reopened in 1990 as a recreation rental and listed in the National Historic Lookout Register on April 1, 1991 as one of the few remaining lookouts in the Siskiyou National Forest.

Snow Camp Lookout is just thirteen air miles from the Pacific Ocean, approximately twenty-six road miles southeast of Gold Beach or thirty-six road miles northeast of Brookings (located in Township 37 South, Range 12 West of the Willamette Meridian, Section 30).

Snow Camp Lookout is available to the public to rent from early June until sometime in October each year, depending on the weather. The Chetco Ranger District begins taking reservations in January for the upcoming year. The minimum age to obtain a permit is twenty-one. The fee in 1996 was $30 per twenty-four hours, running from noon to noon, for a maximum stay of three days. Contact Chetco Ranger District, 555 Fifth Street, Brookings, OR 97415, (541) 469-2196 for further information.

It should be noted that all rental fees collected are used solely to support the lookout. Once you have secured your rental permit, look forward to your stay at Snow Camp with anticipation, for like so many of the good things in life, it seems to pass all too quickly.

The roads to Snow Camp are in good shape, but are winding, with a gravel surface. They can be treacherous, especially if you're not familiar with this type of road. Many people use these roads, including logging trucks, forestry workers, recreational vehicles and others just out for a country drive, so stay to the right and drive defensively. Drive a vehicle that is in good condition with good tires. Flat tires are common. Carry adequate clothing, food and water in the event of an emergency.

Be aware that there are some road closures in effect from October 1 through June 1 each year. This is to prevent the spread of the Port Orford Cedar root disease *(Phytrphora lateralis),* via the mud and dirt on vehicles. This disease is prevalent north of Snow Camp Lookout and threatens uninfected cedar stands to the south.

Approaching Snow Camp from Brookings will give you some opportunities to view the lookout from a distance. The route from Gold Beach offers few glimpses of the lookout. Within one-half mile of the lookout, there is a locked gate to which the Forest Service will have given you the combination along with your rental confirmation letter. Feel free to lock the gate behind you as anyone on official business can gain access at any time. The last half mile to the "parking lot" is rough but fairly level and suitable for a two-wheel drive vehicle, although one with good ground clearance would be best.

There is a road up to the lookout, but it is steep and only suitable for a four-wheel drive vehicle. The Forest Service prefers that people do not drive to the top. The final 200 yards is referred to many times in the journal entries as "the hill." If you packed heavy or brought too much, "the hill" will make you aware of every extra pound. Even with the wheelbarrow made available at the bottom of "the hill," this trek can be no easy task, especially when you consider there is no water available at the lookout and each gallon weighs over eight pounds. It is a time when many wish they had stuck with that vow to exercise regularly.

Once you have made your first trip up the hill, stop to admire the view (and catch your breath). Take in the glistening ocean to the west, the nearby peaks of the Big Craggies Botanical Area and the Kalmiopsis Wilderness. Most would agree that the view makes all the effort, including "the hill," worthwhile.

Inside the cozy little glass house you'll find a double bed, foam mattress, table, chairs, wood stove, woodbox (usually full), two low counters (so the Firefinder's view is unobstructed), and in the center of the room, a stand is bolted to the floor with an Osborne Firefinder attached to it. This instrument has "sights" mounted on a swivel with a map underneath. It allows a lookout to pinpoint a fire in the rugged terrain, sometimes with amazing accuracy.

On the walls are: fire extinguisher, fly swatter (considered by some as a necessity, not a luxury), fire ax, first aid kit, carved signs indicating the various peaks and attractions in every direction, and a much referred to wind gauge, so you can know just how powerful those winds are that seem determined to blow you and the lookout right off the mountain.

Items donated by the occupants include dishes, silverware, dishpan, dishrack, pans, hand towels, broom, dustpan, mop, mop bucket, and sometimes canned food. If you're lucky, the previous tenant left some spare water for you. Water is a precious item at this elevation! Refer to the appendix for a list of other items you may want to bring to the lookout and directions on how to get there.

Outside, there is an elevated catwalk with a railing going all around the lookout. A picnic table sits right outside the steps, and a communications "building" nearby...a fiberglass module with a radio tower next to it. There are also the ends of two buried culverts protruding from the ground which house seismic equipment operated by the U.S. Geological Survey.

Down the path on the ocean side of the ridge is an old outhouse that was lying on its side in 1993. I suspect it was actually blown over by a powerful gust at some time. Below the communications building is a modern fiberglass version of the outhouse, with a much heralded view of the Pacific Ocean. You can leave the door open and have a most fantastic view with little concern that anyone will look back at you. The designer of this facility didn't realize the application of this particular outhouse, as the seat is to the left of center, which forces a body to lean to the right to see the extreme limits of the coastline to the south.

There are other lookouts available to rent throughout the United States and more are being saved and renovated all the time (see Appendix for a list of those available in the Western United States).

ACKNOWLEDGMENTS

I and many others wish to thank the volunteers for their many days of time and effort in preserving these wonderful pieces of history. One such group that especially needs acknowledgment is the Sand Mountain Society of Portland, Oregon, which was instrumental in saving Snow Camp.

A special thanks to the US Forest Service for recognizing the value of these places and their willingness to share them with the public. The cooperation of the Chetco Ranger District in assisting me with the creation of this book was invaluable. [Reference: Heritage Files, Siskiyou National Forest, Chetco Ranger District.]

And finally, let's not forget the renters who kept Snow Camp alive and healthy with their donations, "fix-it" efforts, journal entries and cooperation. I think it should be noted that in six years of rental occupancy, not one act of vandalism has occurred by a renter at Snow Camp. That's the America I like to hear about.

Don't forget to read the journal and write your own entry!

SNOW CAMP LOOKOUT AS VIEWED FROM THE SOUTH

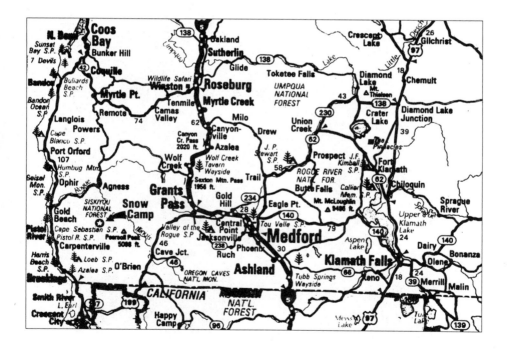

SOUTHWEST OREGON

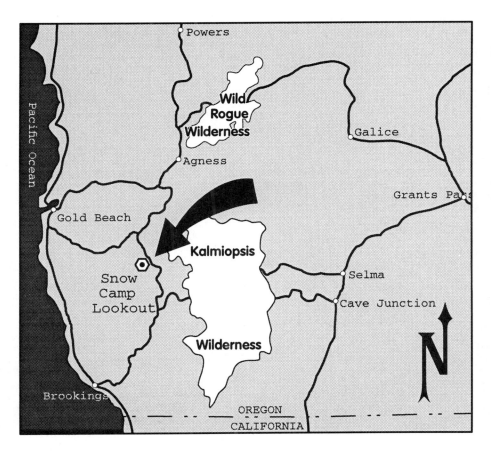

Powers

Wild
Rogue
Wilderness

Galice

Agness

Pacific Ocean

Grants Pass

Gold Beach

Kalmiopsis

Snow
Camp
Lookout

Selma

Cave Junction

Wilderness

Brookings

OREGON
CALIFORNIA

N

REGIONAL MAP

PANORAMIC PHOTOGRAPH

The above is just a portion of a photograph that was originally 39" long by 5" high taken from the roof of Snow Camp Lookout. Between 1933 and 1938, approximately 1600 lookouts and patrol points were visited by any one of six two-man teams with special camera equipment designed to take a 360 degree picture. The purpose was to give the lookout and the dispatcher an identical picture to look at and refer to when plotting a "smoke."

These photographic teams were given top priority for the use of the local packers since clear days were needed for their project. To assure the most unobstructed picture possible, the camera equipment was mounted on the peak of the lookout building, no matter how high up or how windy!

GATE AT THE LOOKOUT...ONE-HALF MILE TO GO!

"Are we there yet?"

SNOW CAMP JOURNAL — 1990

June 16 - Gary and Kathy P.; Brookings, OR

This is the first night the lookout has been used except for fire emergencies since 1972. There was a spectacular sunset tonight but I suppose every sunset and sunrise seen from Snow Camp Lookout is spectacular. Earlier today we ventured over to Game Lake and let the dogs go swimming. We also explored the bottom of the hill near the parking area here at the lookout. To the north are the remains of what we believe was the cabin that the lookouts used prior to the construction of the current building. Ben Gardner told me that the lookout used to spend the night in the cabin and then hike up to the lookout to watch for fires during the day. It is quiet now as we all settle down to bed . There is only the sound of a gentle wind and the noise of the lantern burning. I think the little building is glad to have some company.

June 17 - Laurie and Chris C.-T.; Gold Beach, OR

(Laurie) It's great to be one of the first ones to spend a night here. The flowers are coming out all over, so we need to be careful where we walk. If you listen, you can hear the frogs from the meadow below and the different birds. If you are into clouds, this is the place to be!

(Chris) Spent the day exploring the area. Drove around to Fairview Meadow and wandered around enjoying the open, needle-littered forest. Left Fairview and drove to Game Lake. This area is really fascinating; what a diversity of ecological zones, probably more pronounced in this part of the SNF (Siskiyou National Forest) than most anywhere else.

Saw two fawns with their mother, two additional does (no fawns apparent). Other wildlife as usual: Gray squirrels, various birds and sign of either a bobcat or coyote. Surprised not to have seen any bear sign in today's wanderings. Wildflowers are in bloom now. Saw numerous irises, largely the pale yellow variety but some white, purple and yellow with purple; also saw elegant cat's ears, powdery dudleya, cliff penstenion, Indian paintbrush, mule ears and a variety of unidentified others.

June 29 - Steve M. and party; Brookings, OR

Came here with Steve. Couldn't make it up the hill with our Toyota. Excellent view. Still wish we could stay here longer. My dad brought his telescope to look at the stars with it. My friend got carsick up on the way (I don't blame her). We brought our bikes. It was real fun!

Ended our visit with a hike to Windy Valley. It was a nice day; when we got back we were starving and ate everything in sight. Funny how fresh air and a long hike will make a person so famished. Great place to be.

July 4 - Ruth C.; Eugene, OR

Our party of six (four two-footed and two four-footed), certainly enjoyed the view, after a war of annihilation against the army of ants, which unfortunately look as though they are nesting in the S.W. corner of the lookout. In spite of the usual assorted comments of, "How could I have forgotten that?!" and the consequent adaptations to missing objects (such as pillows, can openers and coffee filters), we spent a quiet night lulled by the stormy sound of the wind. We wondered if the lights in the distance were from Brookings or Crescent City.

Six of the feet (two human, mine, and four canine), are from New York City. Being in Oregon in general, and here in particular, confirms my belief that no one would live there rather than here if they were in their right mind (my dog has no choice; work is my weak excuse). People acclaim New York's impressiveness and I suppose its energy and wealth are, but it represents a completely different set of values/priorities and my bias is that those represented by the beauty of the mountains and the sea are more enduring.

July 6 - Margo H.; Brookings, OR

Brought four girls from Cadet Troop #590. Their first reaction was amazement! The ants were the next reaction. We went to Game Lake and had to wait for three huge elk to clear the road. We saw fourteen deer of various ages, several gray squirrels and chipmunks.

It is very peaceful here but boring for the troops. They've played cards, roasted marshmallows and popped corn. At one point they raced in twos down the hill to the car and back. Susan made it in two minutes, 17 seconds; Shera in two minutes, 40 seconds; Nicki decided to try and made it in one minute, 10 seconds. She's a cross-country champ.

July 8 - Bill and Betsy K.; Pistol River, OR

After packing countless days through the rugged Oregon Coastal Mountains, we finally arrived at our long sought destination, Snow Camp Lookout. Upon meeting the natives, they exclaimed, "Aren't you Bill, the

2

Great Outdoors man, fine figure of a man, hunter par excellence?!" I said "Yes" because I am. Then I proceeded to pass out a cool Coke to everyone. I dug deep into my pack to recover what was left of the 400 pounds of ice I carried to ensure the refreshing drink was cold. The women smothered me in hugs and kisses. I told the men a handshake would be sufficient.

I then unpacked my handy two bit ax, hatchet, saw and splitting maul, hopped off the shear rock face bluff and gathered several cords of firewood for our evening on the mountain. On my way back, I encountered a wild and furosous (yeah, well spelling doesn't count here) beast. Not large in size but it had huge front teeth, a long gray tail and it sat up facing me, hissing and chattering, challenging me to a dual. Keeping calm, I swung my ax about and hollered, "Hah! You slimey dog." It quickly picked up an acorn and vanished into the brush. Another deadly encounter that I pulled through safely. Soon it is time to prepare for a long, adventuresome-filled journey home.

July 10, 11 and 12 - Norman, Jeanne and Amber with dog, "Hershey"; Harbor, OR

A good time was had by all. A wonderful three days. Horseflies every-where! I don't want to leave "Woof, woof, woof."

Our family (plus trusty hound dog), arrived yesterday. After four trips back and forth up the hill lugging our creature comforts (mainly water and food), we paused long enough in the 100+ degree heat to doubt our sanity. Our darling daughters (ages 7 & 3), ran shrieking from the horseflies to the safety of the lookout to discover ants weren't any better! Once we convinced them that we were the intruders, not the other way around and that for everything good there is always a few unpleasant things (like biting bugs), they settled down to serious matters, like chasing lizards and butterflies.

After lunch, we were all hot and tired so we took a drive to explore the area. We found water to play in and saw some really beautiful scenery. After dinner, we retired to the deck to escape the evening sun. Looking east, we watched the thunderclouds build and the shadows grow. The sunset was brilliant and colorful, but living on the coast as we do, we are spoiled to see these types of sunsets time after time. I found myself drawn to the mountains, just staring and watching and wishing I could hear the stories they must harbor. It fascinates me to sit and look at something as old as time itself and try to relive history in my imagination. I am thankful we could bring our children up here for these few days.

We were very fortunate to watch an all-night electrical storm. Spectacu-lar! It was over Collier Butte. The kids thought they were fireworks. Maybe next year we'll come back to this little lookout in the clouds.

July 12 - Mark and Darleen; Portland, OR

After three sweltering trips up the hill and all the horseflies deftly taken care of, we have been able to explore nearby and finally relax. Thanks to everyone who sprayed the ants. We didn't even know they were a problem until we read this journal. It is truly peaceful. The fog is thick over the ocean.

Vistas, sunset, stars and moon are all breathtakingly beautiful, all serenaded by an eerie, ceaseless wind. We were awakened in the middle of the night by a bright moon and an attack of fleas. We aren't sure if we brought them with us or if they were here just waiting for their next victims.

Great recommendation, Lennea.

July 21 - Jane K., Paul B. and John; Eugene, OR

We have felt on top of the world in every way since we arrived Friday evening. This trip has not been without its challenges but we brought most of them with us in the form of our eighteen month old son, John.

When we first arrived, we flung open the three windows for ventilation and then John ran around the deck, promptly hitting his head on each one! Minor mishaps and a few tears aside, we are having a great time.

We traveled yesterday to Game Lake and hiked an hour or so into the Kalmiopsis Wilderness on Horse Sign Trail. We then drove to Redwood Bar on the Chetco River and swam all afternoon.

Here is a list of the plants blooming on the way to and from Game Lake—Shrubs: azalea and rhododendron (waning), some kind of ceonothus, canyon live oak. Flowers: paintbrush (both red and a gorgeous pink), mimubus, tiger lily, stunning pink *Lilium bolanderi*, scarlet fritillaria, many asters, including oxeye and shasta daisies, and more.

July 27 - Gary and Kathy P.; Brookings, OR

Well, here we are again. I knew we would be back. In this visit to the lookout, we brought up the firefinder and set it up to work. This is the same firefinder that was in Snow Camp Lookout in 1972 when Les left. We didn't find any fires however. We also brought up a video camera and took some sweeping scenery shots. Hopefully this film will end up with a snappy narrative dubbed over our fleeting remarks of "Do I push this button?" and "Quick, get out of the way," or "Damn lens cap...always gets in the way!"

Tonight we should see lots of shooting stars. A meteor shower is happening. Last night at 12:30, we saw six shooting stars and two satellites. Then we went back to sleep.

September 2 - The S. Family; Brookings, OR

Everything was perfect, except our two year old.

September 8 and 9 - Seneva S.; Grants Pass, OR

What a view! What serenity, with only the sound of the wind. The fresh air and plants were great. What a way to celebrate "Grandparents Day" and our anniversary, a surprise gift from the children.

September 15 and 16 - Joy Ann D. and Gene J.; Coos Bay, OR

Totally enclosed in a blanket of clouds all day Saturday. Clear night sky with all white just below. Thanks, God.

September 21 and 22 - Gary and Donna F. with son Jesse.

Perfect weather! Fantastic view! Wonderful place! We felt we were on top of the world. We woke up in the morning to a sea of clouds all around us.

September 23 - Andy, Bobbie, Tristan and Ed; Brookings, OR

This morning is a real cloud show in all directions. The sea of clouds at a thousand feet below keeps moving in and out of valleys, over ridges and peaks and even over Snow Camp now and then. Green Craggie and Big Craggies have been above the "sea" level but Bosley Butte keeps coming and going. Collier Butte, Game Lake Peak, Saddle Mountain, Horse Sign Butte and peaks to the northeast are staying above the sea which has captured the Illinois and Rogue River valleys. A pretty view.

September 24 - Fred T. and Jim B.; Anaheim, CA (Disneyland)

We knew we were in trouble when we saw the steep hill we had to climb with a sixty-four quart cooler full of drinks. After four trips we finally lugged all our gear up to the lookout, feeling very humble about our physical capabilities. We were in awe of the view up here. We're used to a gray film of smog and are not sure if we can handle all of this fresh air!

In the evening we were entertained by nature's awesome show of lightning storms. After our delightful gourmet dinner of hamburgers and a vintage crisp beer, we settled down to a comfortable evening of rest and relaxation. Good night. Zzzzzz.

September 28 and 29 - Roger, Val, Duane, Arlynda, Tami and John S.

(Tami) Everyone except mom and I went hunting. Mom tried to make campfire coffee…(Yuck). Sady, our dog, was bored stiff. Just got a report from Duane and Arlynda, "No deer." What a bummer.

The best things for mom and I to do is write in this journal, drink coffee, get hammered, make trips to the outhouse, cook dinner and keep things clean.

This is a super place to camp, very windy but a great place. We are all having a super time. The best part of the whole trip is being together as a family, something we haven't done in a long time!

October 5 and 6 - Tex and Suzanne; Brookings, OR

Came up here Friday afternoon to begin closing up the lookout for the season. What a change from our last visit one month ago. On our last trip here, it was breezy but warm (hot, if you found a protected spot out of the wind). We picked lots of red huckleberries along the road up from the gate, for huckleberry pancakes, and the last of the wildflowers were still in bloom. Last month's full moon and a clear night lit up the lookout as bright as an electric light. This trip up here has been quite different. An east wind has been howling nonstop since our arrival. A very cold wind! By sunset last night, I could see my breath condensing in the cold. The wind has been just incredible, blowing all night long and it is even stronger in the morning. It's as powerful as any Santa Ana wind that I've ever experienced! The entire building is constantly shaking and drafts blow through as if the windows were open. We really appreciated having the wood stove.

The change in the seasons is really evident. The huckleberries are gone, as well as the wildflowers. This month's full moon had an eerie quality to it, with dark clouds flying by its face at an amazing speed, occasionally swarming around the lookout and then dissipating in the wind. No fog in the valleys this morning!

Cleaned all the windows yesterday, 104 panes on the inside and 104 panes outside. Could be a full time job; makes a real difference.

More observations on the wind: The lookout is now shaking so hard that the coffee in my cup, which sits on the table, is threatening to slosh out of the cup! Even the dogs won't stay outside for more than a few minutes and I can see my truck shaking with every gust. Quite an experience!

Well, we're going to finish up our cleaning chores this morning and then bolt for shelter from the wind. Goodbye to Snow Camp for the season. Have a good winter.

That was the last entry for Snow Camp's 1990 season.

6

LOOKOUT ANECDOTES

Joe

Joe was a German who cut trails and spoke broken German. He was working during the time when the Forest Ranger was very strictly enforcing the laws. One day when he was working on the trail to Snow Camp Meadow, he stopped to rest on the trail. He saw the Ranger shoot a deer in Snow Camp Meadow. (Afterwards, they found out it was a doe, not legal to take.) The Ranger having so strictly enforced the hunting regulations sheepishly said, "I guess I made a mistake." Joe replied, "Oh, sometimes I do too."

Bill

Bill Lane, nicknamed "Sourdough Bill," was the lookout for twenty years in the 1930s. He prided himself on his accuracy for spotting fires. One day he reported a smoke to the dispatcher. They sent a crew down to find it but the smoke could not be located. The crew checked with Bill again and he saw the smoke and insisted it was where he said it was. Finally the crew located Bill's "fire." It was two bulls fighting in a road and stirring up a bunch of dust. It was Bill's only mistake in reporting smokes.

Ruby

Ruby VanDevanter, for whom there is a park named after near Smith River, was at the lookout during World War I. Ruby was a botanist and was out looking for plants one day. She heard voices speaking in German nearby. Well, apparently they were trying to put up a radio antenna. Ruby reported the men to the sheriff or Forest Ranger and was told to keep the incident quiet and they'd be right up. The authorities came and caught the spies but the incident was kept top secret. She received an award from the government after the war was over.

THE ACCIDENT REPORT

The scene opens upon a lookout tower person lying in his hospital bed contemplating how he should answer a letter from the Workers Compensation Board. Eventually this was his reply:

I am writing in response to your request for additional information in block #3 of the Accident Report Form. I wrote 'poor planning' as the cause of my accident. You said in your letter that I should explain more fully. I trust that the following details will be sufficient.

I was an Alberta Forest Service tower person. On the day of the accident I was taking my last look off the top of my new 100 foot tower. When I had completed my look, I discovered that I had, over the course of the summer, brought about 300 pounds of books and spare materials to the top. Rather than carry the now unneeded books and materials down by hand, I decided to lower the items down in a small barrel by using a pulley which fortunately was attached to the floor of the cupola.

Securing the rope at ground level, I went to the top of the tower and loaded the books and materials into the barrel. Then I went back to ground level and untied the rope, holding tightly to insure a slow descent of the 300 pounds of books. You will note in block #11 of the Accident Report that I weigh only 155 pounds.

Due to my surprise at being jerked off the ground so suddenly, I lost my presence of mind and forgot to let go of the rope. Needless to say, I proceeded at a rather rapid rate of speed up the side of the tower. In the vicinity of the fifty foot level, I met the barrel coming down. This explains my fractured skull and broken collarbone. Slowed only slightly, I continued my rapid ascent, not stopping until the fingers of my right hand were two knuckles deep into the pulley.

Fortunately by this time, I had regained my presence of mind and was able to hold onto the rope in spite of all my pain. At about the same time, however, the barrel of books hit the ground and the bottom fell out of the barrel. Devoid of the weight of the books, the barrel now weighed about twenty pounds. As you might imagine, I made a rapid descent down the side of the tower. In the vicinity of the fifty foot level, I met the barrel

8

coming up. This accounts for my two fractured ankles and lacerations of my legs and lower body.

The encounter with the barrel slowed me enough to lessen my injuries when I fell onto the pile of books, and fortunately only three vertebrae were cracked. I am sorry to report, however, that as I lay there on the books in severe pain, unable to stand or move in any way and watching the barrel 100 feet above me, I once again lost my presence of mind...I let go of the rope.

THE JAPANESE ATTACK ON OREGON

My thanks to Ray Kresek for allowing me to use the following story from his book *Fire Lookouts of Oregon and Washington.*

Howard Gardner awoke at dawn as usual on Wednesday, September 9, 1942. From his lookout house atop Mount Emily, seven miles northeast of Brookings, he glanced out over a sea of billowing fog. Only the peaks and ridge tops jutted above the mist that morning. The twigs and evergreen needles were still dripping after a heavy rain. The fire danger was virtually nil...for the moment.

As Gardner was about to strike the match to light his wood stove in preparation for breakfast, there came a strange airplane out of the southeast. As it chugged past the lookout, he didn't recognize it, nor did he see any numbers or markings on it. Certainly, it was not a type he had ever seen or heard before.

At 6:24 A.M. Gardner's voice flashed over the radio speaker at Gold Beach Ranger Station forty miles away: "Gold. This is five-six. Reporting one aircraft. Single engine. With pontoons. Type unknown. Flying low. Seen. East, two miles. Was circling. Now headed northwest."

The operator on duty at Gold Beach relayed the routine report to the Roseburg Air Filter Center; then everybody went about their day's business.

9

Seven miles east of Mount Emily, Keith Johnson was still in the fog at his Bear Wallow Lookout. After breakfast, he went "ten-seven" for the rest of the morning to brush out the ridge trail.

When the fog cleared out of the valleys at noon, Gardner noticed one thin patch of bluish white remaining four miles toward the southeast. With his binoculars, he confirmed that it was indeed smoke. Not much...but nonetheless a forest fire.

Cross shots from Bear Wallow and **Snow Camp** Lookouts placed it in the NW ¼ of Section 22, Township 40 South, Range 12 West; at the 1700' level of Wheeler Ridge.

District ranger Ed Marshal dispatched Gardner and Johnson, who would converge from cross country to the fire with their smokechaser packs.

The blaze was soon under control at less than a tenth of an acre. However, in a circle fifteen yards across were numerous small chunks of some type of burning chemical. Near the middle was a small crater. Several trees had been sheared off...as if by a bomb. Further inspection revealed fragments of a metal casing. It was a bomb!

The firemen immediately reported in on their portable radio set, giving the district ranger all the details...sketchy as they were. When he advised Roseburg that one of its military planes had lost a bomb over the Siskiyou Forest, the phone rang back an hour later demanding more information. Next, it was the FBI, wanting to know still more.

As they continued mopping up and sifting the scene, Gardner and Johnson found fifty pounds of metal fragments, including a tail fin. On it was an inscription...in Japanese!

Throughout the next week the woods around Mount Emily and Wheeler Ridge were crawling with FBI agents, newspaper reporters and army troops. Since the army had taken down all the road signs in order to confuse any potential invaders, nearly everyone became lost and none of them found the bomb area.

Twenty years after the war ended, the real story became public. Nubuo Fujita was the pilot of the airplane and the invited guest at the 1962 Brookings Azalea Festival.

After Pearl Harbor was bombed, the Japanese submarines began harassing ships along the coast of California, Oregon and Washington. Nubuo Fujita's submarine and others like it began their sporadic raids on merchant ships and onshore outposts, causing near panic in coastal residents. Rumors of imminent attack circulated across the nation, while our fighting troops continued to be shipped overseas by the thousands, leaving few to defend our homeland. Naturally, our Defense Department kept all records of such raids top secret.

Of all the Japanese subs, Fujita's crew was daring beyond belief. In addition to its normal complement of torpedoes, the sub carried a small disassembled seaplane which was put together topside after the sub had surfaced. Therefore, its missions meant a potential kamikaze for every member of the crew since the vessel was committed to the surface for long periods of time while the seaplane was assembled and disassembled for each flight.

Thus, Fujita's submarine, the I-25, was one of the most vulnerable vessels on the seas as it sat poised due west of the California-Oregon line at forty-two degrees north latitude on the morning of September 9, 1942 — the day the Japanese bombed the Siskiyou National Forest.

These daring attacks on the Pacific Northwest were ingenious and should have been very effective. They surely would have taxed the limited resources and manpower of the times. But as luck would have it, the month of September in 1942 was an unusually wet period in Oregon, allowing small crews to smother Japan's attack on the American homeland.

LESTER WILLIAMS

The following account was written by Lester Williams who was the last person to reside a summer season in Snow Camp lookout as a "lookout," i.e., a person who has the job of regularly looking for "smokes" (fires) and reporting their location as accurately as possible. Lester spent the summer of 1972 at Snow Camp. The lookout was only used intermittently after that time until the restoration began in 1989 and it was available to the public as a rental in June 1990.

_____

Isolation, solitude, loneliness, seclusion and adventure are all terms which can be used to describe the life of a lookout. I say this because the lonely life of being secluded from the rest of the world is the life of a lookout.

11

From my point of view, I think that it takes a special type of person to be a lookout. One that can adjust to the idea of being alone for days, or maybe even weeks. For me, I would say this is quite a change, especially when you consider that I am from a large family and have lived in the city all my life. I guess it is because of the change it offers me, that I enjoy being a lookout. It is a change from constantly running to and from town and from place to place. It offers me a chance to think over my past mistakes and study for the future. And especially since I am a junior in college, this quiet life of a lookout gives me a chance to study for courses that I will take this coming year in school.

The job of being a lookout is very important, perhaps one of the most important jobs in the fire control area of the Forestry Service. The primary purpose is to detect and report fires. This is very important when you consider that at some times fire danger is very high and in case there is a fire, the suppression crew cannot work unless it is reported, in most cases by the lookout.

I think that the job of being a lookout also involves public relations. This is true because in some areas there are many campgrounds close to a lookout. If these lookouts are easily accessible, they are constantly visited by people of many walks of life. My two summers as a lookout brought me into contact with a 4-H Saddle Club, two troops of Boy Scouts, motor scooter riders, doctors, college professors, psychiatrist, loggers and many campers. To me this is a great experience because it offers a variation of the occupations of the people in this area. However, the two Englishmen from Peterbourough (Petersberg) and Rochester, England, would rank among the most rare of my visitors. Also, there have been several from upstate and out of state.

Although he has the same responsibilities as the earlier lookouts, the modern day lookout does not have quite the difficulties. Automation has brought about a change, bringing into existence transistor radios, record players and portable televisions. The kitchen appliances are also updated. With the installation of the butane stove and refrigerator, accommodations are almost like home. There are some lookout stations which have generators for electricity. This is quite a change.

In closing, I will say that being a lookout has been quite an experience. I feel lucky to have had the chance to be one before

aerial coverage completely takes over.
As a Texan, I am not used to forest fires, and would be very
startled to wake up some night with the forest afire around me.
So let us strive to keep the forest green and growing.

Lester Williams, 1972, Snow Camp Lookout

BRUSH MOUNTAIN

When the ex-sailor, Dan Pederson, came to Brush Mountain in southern Oregon in 1913 to serve as the lookout, all he had to work with was a telephone and a crude map stand. But Dan was a man of extraordinary talents and, not content with these rudimentary arrangements, set about creating a better vantage point. Just below the top of the peak was a tall red fir. With such simple tools as an ax, auger and a pair of pliers, Dan began the job of turning this tree into a lookout that when finished would stand 104 feet, which was a good sixty feet above the top of the mountain.

Starting at ground level, he drilled holes one foot deep into the tree in a spiral fashion every eighteen inches into which he drove yew wood pegs. Sitting on the last driven peg, he would drill his next hole into which he would drive a two inch diameter step. He then fastened the ends of the pegs with limber fir poles and wire. When finished in 1916, Dan had created a spiral staircase that circled the peeled and limbed tree four times, with a five foot diameter "crow's nest" at the top.

Included was a firefinder mounted on rollers that could revolve around the crow's nest. When smoke was spotted, Dan would level the firefinder and orient it on Mt. Pitt (presently Mt. McLaughlin) which was due north. With a sly grin, he would explain the procedure to visitors almost apologetically and how it "only took a few seconds."

For the first few years the telephone was located at the bottom of the tree, so it took valuable time to descend to report a smoke. Not satisfied with this delay, he constructed a homemade elevator by rigging two buckets to a cable with a pulley and counterbalancing his

13

weight with rocks. With a simple pull on the cable, Dan would go shooting up to his crow's nest or back down again with ease.

Visitors would clutch the rungs of the ladder in a slow hair-raising ascent. However, one day when no one was looking, a young boy weighing half as much as Dan, climbed into the empty bucket and pulled the pin releasing the similar bucket filled with rocks from the top of the tree. The lad began to shoot to the top and was sure to be launched into space when Dan saved him by gripping the cable with his bare hands which served as brakes. The lad was not hurt but Dan suffered severe rope burns.

Pederson was also a master craftsman at building log houses with tight fitting, beveled corners. A dozen cabins in the area were built by him, all with those distinctive tight fitting corners in which water could not accumulate to rot the logs. Because of a shortage of timber near the top of Brush Mountain, he constructed a cozy stone house for himself, complete with an artistic fireplace and a thatched roof.

Today, little remains of the genius of Dan Pederson but the site where he created his impressive accomplishments has been nominated to the National Register of Historic Places in memory of an amazing Norwegian sailor.

Author's Note: The story of Brush Mountain is from Carroll Brown's *History of the Rogue River National Forest,* Vol. 1, 1970, and Ray Kresek's *Fire Lookouts of Oregon and Washington,* 1985.

APPROACHING SNOW CAMP LOOKOUT

"The Hill"

SNOW CAMP JOURNAL — 1991

June 15, 16 and 17 - Steve and Tina R., Jack and Cheryl M. with dog, Jodie; Grants Pass, OR

(Steve) There are four of us in our group. We arrived yesterday afternoon. I brought my video camera hoping to get pictures of the ocean and stars at night. No such luck, foggy and overcast most of the time. We noticed ponds and Snow Camp Meadow from the lookout but couldn't find it in the car. Today we will hike there.

I woke up this morning (Father's Day) to be told by my wife, "We're going to have a baby!" My first. What a day to be told!

(Jack) On the way here, we witnessed a red-tailed hawk brushing along the road frantically trying to pick up a little rabbit but we surprised him and he dropped it. So we went down the road in hopes of seeing him return...no such luck. He circled around and saw us and flew off.

After Steve and Tina left, Cheryl and I took a drive to Game Lake. It was as breathtaking as the other entries in the journal had described it. On the way back, we ventured off on many of the little roads. We located a trail on the map that would take us down to Hurt Cabin. If we only had known how much it would **hurt** getting there. It was a very steep trail. The climb almost did me in. Didn't think I was going to make it. Cheryl climbed right out without any problem. I was amazed by her endless energy. I was so glad to see our home on top of the mountain. It was a welcome sight. We have to leave tomorrow. Not looking forward to going back to reality.

June 17 and 18 - Kris and Craig T.; Eugene, OR

The wind was blowing very hard all night. I love the sound of the wind. It is very comforting to sleep by. This is really a fantastic place. All lookouts such as these should be protected for their historical and cultural value. They are as much a part of the forest as the trees themselves.

As a forestry major soon to be at Oregon State University, I really enjoy studying the ecology and geology of the area. It is especially interesting to study the vast areas that were burned over by forest fires many years ago and to see areas in many different stages of ecological succession. As a mountain-eer and wilderness lover, I spend hours visually exploring the Kalmiopsis Wilderness from this high vantage point. This is an area I would like to spend a lot of time backpacking through, exploring the canyons, mountains and botanical diversity.

This is a fantastically beautiful place and my wife and I plan to return very soon. We had a wonderful time.

June 20 and 21 - Karen T. and Susan; Corvallis, OR

(Karen) Woke to a beautiful sunrise. Watched it and dozed off. Up again at seven. Had a scrumptious breakfast of Cream of Wheat in the beautiful sunshine. Clear, lovely, quiet and warm. Decided to check out Windy Valley and kept on going. On the way back we followed a trail around the southeast side of Snow Camp. Came all the way around to the west side and decided to head back. Got to the rock formations on the south side of Snow Camp Mountain and Sue decided she wanted to come up cross-country. I don't recommend it. Lots of tan oak and chaparral, over my head (five feet, one inch). Thick as can be. Our legs look like we have been tortured. The pollen was terrible from the tan oak, etc. No place for someone with allergies. Left at 9:30, back at 4 P.M. Rested, munched out and drank several quarts of water. Then decided to find Game Lake and got lost. Will coast downhill going out tomorrow to conserve gasoline. We are having fun! It is about 8 P.M. and the clouds are forming a sea around us. It looks like the *Neverending Story*. Beautiful.

(Susan) Now it's my turn. I cannot believe how utterly breathtaking the view of our world is from this small lookout. It makes a person glad to be alive and healthy enough to traverse this ground. We saw some beautiful flowers: Indian paintbrush, sedum, pussy ears, bear's grass, violets, rhodo-dendrons, azaleas, Pacific starflowers and several we were unable to identify. Discovered a small creek below Windy Valley and stepped over one bear sign. And yes, I do admit to miscalculating (slightly) the height of the oak and chaparral. I also do not recommend a cross-country climb.

The sun setting over the top of the sea of marshmallow cream clouds in the valleys around our mountaintop was awesome. We have had two excel-lent days, couldn't ask for better weather. It will be sad to leave tomorrow.

(Karen) The only disappointing item in our stay here has been the unsightly patches from clear-cutting. Hopefully one day we all will learn the importance of recycling and then the number of these patches will not be so great. This is truly a unique place.

June 22 - Jack G., Linda D. and party; Coos Bay, OR

We arrived about 1:30 P.M. to find a neat lookout on top of the mountain, much classier than we expected. What a view...always changing every few minutes. Such fun to watch all the weather patterns.

It's wonderful to be without telephone or TV, just the sounds of the wind. Thanks to the Forest Service and the volunteers who have made this so comfortable.

June 26 - Linda and Amy B. and Ben and Angela K., George D.; Crescent City, CA and Campbell, CA

(Linda) After following the never ending trail, we finally made it up to the lookout at about 2:30 P.M. I have brought my daughter (8), my niece (9), two nephews (14 and 15) and our dog. Before we even made it to the lookout, one slipped by the old mine and we thought he was a goner.

I started a fire this morning and have been reading through the stories and articles we found in the cabin. They are great! They give you the feel of the area and the people who have stayed here. Looking at the mountains surrounding me, I wonder how anyone ever made it through to the coast to settle this land.

(Amy) My name is Amy B. I came up here with my mom. When I first started up the hill, I thought it was going to be easy but I was wrong. We played a game of hide and seek, we chased lizards and we also found an old dump. I saw a snake go into a hole. The fog is slowly passing by. I really had fun up here and I would like to come back soon.

June 28 and 29 - Mark and Joy L.; Bandon, OR

The first place our kids had to check out was the "restroom facilities." After one check, they decided they would rather go in the bushes. Shawna (9) and Kyle (8) then decided to go exploring and look for Indian arrowheads. They only found rocks which I suppose we will have to pack all the way home. Krista (4) and Tyler (2) didn't venture too far but also found "treasures" to bring home.

After dinner we played cards and watched the sun slowly set. When the sun finally disappeared, we laid in bed and began counting stars and boat lights. We could also see lights from town. Finally, everyone fell asleep. Yeah! An hour or so later, I awoke to a huge full moon which lit up the entire area. It was beautiful! There were some clouds below the lookout. It was like we were in heaven looking down.

When morning came we ate breakfast and were off for an adventure. We drove down to Fairview Meadow just in time to see a herd of about thirty elk crossing the road. They were huge and the one bull had velvet on his antlers.

It became so foggy, we couldn't see very far ahead so we turned around trying to find a trail to Windy Valley. (Never did).

We then drove up the road to find Game Lake. We stopped the pickup by Game Lake Trail and hiked for about a mile. It seemed like five miles with the kids! It was still very foggy and we never found the lake. It would have been peaceful, I think, but we couldn't hear the "peace" over the kids crying. Krista wanted to go back to our "motel." When we reached the pickup it was dead, so we had to push it (forever) to get it started.

Back at the lookout, we ate lunch and decided to take the kids somewhere else before they killed each other. The fog is so thick we can't see more than 20 or 30 feet. We are beginning to go stir crazy. I would like to come back again when the kids are a little older (and there is no fog).

Dave, Michelle, Meliah, Cameron and Laramie. If you read this, we hope you have a good time and don't get lost. We would tell you where everything is, but we never found anywhere we planned to.

June 30 and July 1 - Greg and Melissa S. with son Marty, Dwight and Marie S.; Medford and Coos Bay, OR

The sun is hanging just above the Pacific ocean, ready to take its evening bath. The final rays give off a romantic copper glow.

Our eleven month old son, Marty, began walking today. He has done one or two steps before, but today he went six steps before going down.

July 3, 4, 5 and 6 - Hank and Sue L.; Coos Bay, OR

(Hank) Sue and I arrived at 8:30 P.M. on the 3rd of July. I am glad we brought the wheelbarrow, it made the pack up the hill soooo easy!!

Member of local indigenous population visited during breakfast. Came in through the open window left of the door. Sue cleaned up several torpedo shaped calling cards left by our breakfast visitor.

(12:54 P.M.) Noticed a lot of smoke to the north and slightly west. Have seen borate bomber aircraft come and go at approximately 11:20 A.M. Hope it is under control.

(July 4 - Sue 8:46 P.M.) Had wonderful chicken stir-fry with veggies. Hank forgot soy sauce but was very good anyway. Returned from short walk to find breakfast visitor inside an empty peanut snack bag. Left another calling card upon departure. Fire still seems to be burning to the north-northwest. I hope this wind calms soon. I know the firefighters are having trouble with containment. Hope to see some fireworks tonight, either in Brookings or Carpenterville.

(Hank - 8:57 P.M.) Sue insisted that I recheck the wind velocity. I stood between the lookout and the communications building. The wind was 40 to 45 mph with gusts up to 50 mph. I think I'll not stand on the deck when I check it again.

(July 5) I woke up at 3 A.M. this morning and had to take care of some pressing business. While I was out, it occurred to me that the wind seemed more intense. Through the night, the wind has been 40 to 45 mph and now at 5:19 A.M., it has increased to 50 to 55 mph with gusts up to 60 mph. The wind direction is from the east-northeast. I wonder if any of the previous visitors have experienced strong east winds like these?

Sue is being a good sport about all this attention to the weather. I hope this wordy offering is received in the same spirit. Thank you.

We were a little worried about the kids who were due to visit. At about 3 P.M. a gray pickup drove up to the parking area below. I went to check and it was our daughter, Angel. She had hitched a ride from where our son Scott's car was parked with—believe it or not—three flat tires. After blocking it up and removing the two flats from the car and the flat spare, we proceeded to Gold Beach. On the way there, we changed a flat on my pickup. After replacing my flat with a new tire and also replacing two of Scott's tires, we are now snug in the lookout and looking forward to reading ourselves to sleep.

While we were in Gold Beach spending a considerable amount on three new tires and having a fourth fixed, my thoughts were of the sanctuary of this lookout.

I didn't do a complete weather check this evening. However, I did check the wind velocity and it was 45 to 50 mph with one gust as high as 65 mph. We are getting used to the lookout shaking and hardly notice it anymore.

(July 6) We napped and I finished a book Sue bought me while we were in Gold Beach bolstering the local economy.

I have mentioned the wind quite often but I would like to put it into perspective with the rest of our stay. It, the wind, has amounted to a trivial annoyance compared to the overall wonder and beauty of this lookout.

(July 7 - Sue) The wind was a bit worrisome the first three nights. The 40 to 60 mph had me asking God to please keep us from blowing off the mountain during the night! It is interesting the different perspective from daylight compared to nighttime. The wind is much easier to tolerate during the daylight hours.

The sunrises and sunsets have been so beautiful, and the moonrise just as special. It's wonderful to view the mountains and trees and ocean and sky!

The best part about being up here for four days has been no telephone, no television, no other people and no stress of home and jobs.

This was an anniversary gift from Hank and it has been one of the best ever. Today we have to go back to the real world. It's too bad man has complicated life so much. At least we have these special places to come and appreciate the gifts of our earth. Thank you, Hank.

July 7 and 8 - Mick and Dan O.; Gasquet, CA

(Mick) Evening windy, days spectacular. Fixed door latch, scraped paint off windows. We two men were entertained by three boys, 6, 9 and 11. Somehow found Game Lake, appreciated fewer flies here. Boys ate pizza, candy, soda pop, other great gastro. Played *Skip-bo*, laughed, enjoyed. Tried to leave it a little better than we found it. Added sight wires to Osborne Range Finder, properly oriented azimuth, drank coffee. Wildlife sightings: housemouse in woodbox.

(Dan) It sure does get windy up here, especially around 8:30 to noon. On the way up here, I almost went skydiving with an air mattress. Beautiful sunrise. Hate to leave my brother, Jim. So many things unsaid. I sure do love him.

July 10, 11 and 12 - Larry D., Lisa M. and Ryan N.; Coos Bay, OR

(Larry) Started out right on track, then overshot Snow Camp road by four miles. We ended up at Game Lake turnoff. So, still unsure, we went towards the lake. We stopped about half way to the lake and I walked up the road one-half mile while Lisa and Ryan stayed at the trail head. Around one corner, I came upon the most scary lapping noise on the left side of the road. In my mind, it sounded large enough to be a bear. So there I stood, hearing what I thought was a bear drinking water right next to the shaking Larry. When "he" kept drinking after one and a half minutes without stopping, I then noticed the culvert on the right side of the road and worked on lowering my heart rate.

The sunset on the 10th was molten red. On the 11th we hiked down to Snow Camp Meadow. Saw three elk and two young ones in the meadow. Saw incredible stars at night. Humbling. Four or five shooting stars, one of which was a vertical explosion. Found a 1945 penny at the old structure down by our car. We had a terrific time and plan to return when time allows to the hideout on the mountain.

(Ryan, age 7) I saw a mouse in the woodbox. We chased him out the door. He ran fast. I said, "Get out of here, you pesky rat."

We went down a trail. It was very, very hot! I didn't like the flies or the bees. There were too many! The flies were big! But the stay was fun and we found where the old, old Snow Camp Lookout was. It was very, very fun.

July 12 and 13 - Virginia B. and Jill S.; Crescent City, CA

Mom and I arrived Friday. Beautiful, warm day that got hotter after our sixth trip up the hill. The wind was only a breeze and welcomed as it cooled us. We were impressed by the whole place. The lookout holds so many items of comfort, such as the stove, table, chairs and nice bed. The 360 degree view is beyond description. The fog lays over the coast and spills into the valleys. The sunset last night was pretty, but disappeared into the fog before it hit the horizon.

Date unknown - Dave B., Meliah, Cameron and Laramie; Florence, OR

This a tale that must be told,
A tale both lengthy and true,
Of Meliah the daughter and Cameron, the son,
And little Laramie too.
With them and their mother we got here,
The clouds were hung low all about,
So we got set to start up a fire,
But we first hadda kick the mouse out.
It had taken forever to get here,
'Cause we had been lost half the day,
Till we got set straight by a ranger,
Whom we'd found camping out on the way.
Well he sure was a nice enough fella,
And I'll thank him till my days are done,
Because if he hadn't of helped us,
We couldn't have had so much fun.
The first day turned out pretty casual,
We were all pretty tired that night,
It took us a while to get settled,
And my wife didn't pack very light.
But we ate like a pig up in heaven,
Because of all the good stuff she did bring,
And though the weather was cloudy and windy,
We were as happy as any old king.
Laramie scared us a little,
When she fell offa' the deck,
But the fall didn't do her no damage,
Though it shoulda' broke her fool neck.
That's the way things are with a baby,
The way they always will be,
You could tell not ten minutes later,
That she thought it was all history.
The sun didn't set, the moon didn't rise,
The stars all stayed hidden from sight,

Yet sometime while we were all sleeping,
The rain snuck away with the night.
In the morning the sun rose bright,
So we too rose and fixed us a feast,
And we watched the mist rise from the valley,
Rapidly heading back off to the east.
Well, we saw the ocean and mountains,
And began to think what we might do,
My wife, she came up with some ideas,
And the kids both came up with a few.
We decided we would all go a swimming,
In the hole they had named Panther Lake,
But I'd left my map at the tower,
Let me tell you that was a mistake.
We found us a large herd of elk,
They all looked so pretty and proud,
And we found us some quail,
Some buzzards and hawks,
And we drank from a stream cold n' loud.
We saw us that same ranger fella,
We waved and we bid him adieu,
And we drove, and we drove and we
drove and we drove,
Till the tower had faded from view.
At last we gave up our searching,
We turned and we headed back here,
The plan now was to pick up the map,
And look for something more near.
We did stop and hike down to the meadow,
The one you can see down below,
Let me be the one to tell ya,
It's a real nice place to go.
Now Cameron he saw him a grizzly,
Meliah she saw a buffalo,
They saw them a cougar, a bobcat, a mink,
And a half dozen Sasquatch or so.
Well I won't say that they didn't see them,
Though they all did escape from my view,
But I've gotten older and slower,
No longer quite sure just what's true.
In the mid-afternoon we all wandered,
Back here to our room with a view,
And we sat and we looked at the scenery,
And made us a picture or two.
Then we walked down the hill to explore,
We all had us a very nice time,
The kids poked around and they found stuff,
And then back up the hill we did climb.

24

There was our old friend the good ranger,
His girlfriend was there at his side,
We talked for a bit, then off they did go,
Headed down the mountain's steep side.
I chopped up some wood for a fire,
My wife chopped some stuff for a stew,
The kids all just chopped on each other,
Cause they had nothing better to do.
Then we ate and we waited for sunset,
I read aloud from a book on the shelf,
And their mom made the kids some s'mores,
Cause they were too tired to do it their self.
Soon the sun it fell out of the heaven,
It set the whole ocean on fire,
Then the stars flickered on by the millions,
It's a sight I will always admire.
When it gets dark out came the candles,
And I read till the children all slept,
Then I blew out the lights and I wondered,
About the secrets this mountain kept.
And I happened to wake around midnight,
As the moon was just touching the vine,
It turned blood red then wavered, then vanished,
And made the world seem so quiet and divine.
When the sun rose it turned red all around us,
Though it finally popped up in the east,
And the wind it roared up from the canyon,
Like some kind of tormented beast.
But here in our cabin it was cozy,
And while it seemed pleasant and fine,
I heard that wind scream and I understand,
How a poor man could go outta his mind.
By Dave B.

July 19, 20 and 21 - Michael J. and Marlo M.; Brookings, OR

Everything was very nice when we arrived. Someone left corn and apples. We went down to Snow Camp Meadow. It's like stepping into a different world. Everything tastes better and I slept better than at home.

Several times we talked about leaving the city (Brookings, ha, ha), and moving to the wilderness. I wonder if this place does that to everyone? We saw tiny chipmunks and flies about the same size as the chipmunks. We saw a hawk prowling the meadow and many grouse, tiny baby ones and the mother played hurt to draw our attention away from her babies.

We had some camp crashers. Bruce B. and a friend with two dogs just strolled right in and hung around. Shattered my peace a little.

July 21, 22 and 23 - Andrews and Wilson; Gold Beach, OR

We were the lucky ones because we saw the absolute worst and the best of the toilet. The guys came up today and cleaned it! Yee haa!

Anyway, we're not telling you all everything we did up here but we made the most of it. As a former "lookout" on yonder lookout, Bosley Butte (1982 and 1983), I thoroughly enjoyed being up here with no responsibilities, but the memories sure flooded back...so sweet.

(7:23 A.M.) We had an amazing storm to watch for over four hours last night; covered a length of 75 to 100 miles east of us, north to south lightning, was profuse and profound! The sunset added a rainbow to the storm. West was a spectacular sunset, east was a spectacular large thunderstorm. At 3 A.M. I woke to "mouse goings on" and looked out to see a red three quarter moon setting over the ocean.

Thanks to all the volunteers, donations and considerate inhabitants of this abode.

July 23, 24 and 25 - M. and G.

What a view! What a wind! This cabin shook with the wind during the night. Emptying the gray water in the old toilet was pretty funny. You had to walk backwards out the door and down the steps or it would all blow out.

OLD LEANING OUTHOUSE

26

July 26 and 27 - Michael and Kathy S.; Crescent City, CA

We loved it. The wind never stopped, it let up for fifteen minutes but it didn't stop. We had a mouse, it carried off the dog's food and kept me up half the night. We had a flat tire. Found it last night when we took a walk back down "that" hill. It was a full moon this weekend and it never did get black in here. The best sunsets I have ever seen! We hope to do this again next year.

July 28 - Ted and Megan S.; North Bend, OR

Megan and I are most pleased with the lookout and also with the condition of the lookout. To find a clean house with extra candles, utensils, cups, dishes, matches, etc., not to mention all the firewood...speaks of consideration, one to another. How refreshing it is not to expend the energy to try to fix or repair something the "general public" has kicked up on in a recreational environment.

How nice and pleasant this little house is, sitting on the ridge facing the Big Craggies. How serene and peaceful! Guess you can figure out that I am enjoying this part of my vacation.

A big thank you to whoever left the wheelbarrow. Because it was here, I was able to get the cooler up the hill.

Megan (five years old), has named the mouse "Sandra." Don't worry, we are not going to intentionally feed it.

A word of caution: Where you park your car is a trailhead sign that says 1½ miles—don't believe it. We walked at least three miles before turning back.

If you find Megan's sweatshirt, please leave it at the lookout for another kid to use. Enjoy!

August 1, 2, 3 and 4 - Dick, Peggy, Matthew and Stevie Kay V., and Barb S. and Tasha (dog); North Bend, OR

Our first night was an experience. The mouse only came out once to check us out. Tasha scared it off. Saw one meteor that went down in the ocean.

Our daughter, Stevie, who is three, will not use the outhouse. What an experience. She has trouble with a can. She really likes running around and around the deck. She has the open windows down pat. She tilts her head out of the way as she runs by. Matt, our eight year old, is bored. He has shot all the .22 shells we brought and it's too hot to hike today...poor kid.

We had a good plan. We left our lawn chairs halfway up the hill to the lookout and could sit down and rest while carrying all our stuff up.

August 8 - Roger, Donna, B.J. and Dan S.; North Bend, OR

We hiked to Snow Camp Meadow and enjoyed the animal tracks we saw. The only animals we saw were birds and the two legged variety, a group of hikers heading for Windy Valley. On the way back, my husband and the boys decided to blaze a trail straight up the mountain. What could I do? I followed them up. It was quite an adventure, one I don't wish to repeat soon.

Later we went swimming. We drove down to the river to a great spot. On the way we saw a large black bear run across the road; what a treat!

This morning it's fogged again but the sun is trying mighty hard to burn it off. I wish we could stay longer but we have to head back. This has been the highlight of the summer and I can't wait to do this again.

August 9 - Tarah and Sue W., Toya N., Asuka K., Brenda and Beth H.; Coos Bay and North Bend, OR

We are a Camp Fire group of fourteen year old girls.

The best view was from the can. Sometimes it was the only peaceful spot on this little knoll.

The falling stars were spectacular.

Eighty mile an hour winds are not my idea of fun. The wind howled all night, the building shook. We watched a rat run around the deck railings.

Liked the view of distant Crescent City, Brookings and ships at sea.

As the sun dimmed past the clouds, the four girls took pictures from the sani-can of their liberated bras that hung from the antlers above the door.

Little did they know this would be the last sane moment of their young lives. At the stroke of midnight, their mild mannered leader rose as though in a trance and walked slowly to the door. She picked up the ax and swung around. In her eyes, the girls could see a flicker of her dangerous alter ego personality, "Martha." She ferociously stalked down the stairs with the ax swung over her shoulder. She screeched a horrifying six heart stopping words, "SHUT UP AND GO TO SLEEP!" By those six words, the four girls now knew Martha had once again come out. The only remedy was to sing camp fire songs. If Martha ever appears while you're here, sing the following song which will scare her and any other life-form away:

I wuv a wabbit, a cwazy, cwazy wabbit,
Hop hop bunny,
Bunny, hop hop,
He don't wike cawwots,
I'm crazy over cawwots,
Chew chew, bunny, bunny,
Chew chew, bunny, bunny,

Chew chew, ho, ho.
And when I go to beddy by,
I kiss he, and he kiss I,
But if he's been a such and such,
He has to sleep in his wabbit hutch.
Oh I wuv a wabbit, a cwazy...etc.

Best riddance to you and the mice, who come out at night regularly (there are hundreds of them)! Actually, I didn't see a one, but heard about them.

"This was neat," says our Japanese exchange student.

August 10 - Guy, Alice, Glen, Grant and Kathy T.; Crescent City and Arcata, CA

(Glen) There was hardly a breath of wind until the sun started to set and now it's blowing like mad (8:37 P.M.). Mom, of course, is a little concerned.

I spent most of the day crashing through the brush searching for my dream, an old, old untouched dump. My hopes started to rise when I found a beautiful old purple tinted insulator with a "California" embossed on it. There are also millions of tin cans and a few modern bottles down there (directly beneath us), so if anyone else shares my dream, I wish you the best of luck. Oh, a word of warning, there are lots of red ants down there, so watch out. I only came up with a 1950s Pepsi bottle and a "Log Cabin" tin in pretty good shape.

It's almost beyond words, the beauty here. It serves as a great reminder that we must always preserve places such as this. The only "critter" we saw today was a greenish hummingbird that buzzed in and tried to exit via the closed window. My dad gently picked up the hyper little bird and set him (or her) loose, outside.

August 11, 12 and 13 - Bryon and Dori N.; Yoncolla, OR

(Bryon) After hearing about the lookout rental program in March, we planned our vacation and here we are. I had been here many years ago in the 1970s, just exploring the country. The "hill" to the lookout is the same only I'm older and wiser. After four trips up the "hill," it was 4:30 P.M. and we settled in for our first night.

Before dinner, I read from the journal and the book *Fire Lookouts of the Northwest.* For dinner, it was pasta salad and the view. Our first sunset was as others before had seen, like nothing ever seen from the valleys or towns and cities they came from. As the sun begins to set, the mountains to the east begin to change with the dusk. They take on a new look.

(Dori) My first observation of the lookout was exactly what it contained in the way of survival. Then I knew just how much we needed to haul up the hill and believe me, anything unnecessary stayed with the vehicle. Coming up that "hill," loaded, was pure HELL!

August 16 - Mary and Jennifer and Laura S. and Bronwyn; Pistol River, OR

(Jennifer) I'm eight years old. We saw red hackel berys. I loved the bathrom. I love it hear. I had funn. My birthday is May 2nd. I live in Pistel River. My mom worcks at the forest serves. My mom's name is Mary S. We saw a lot of fog. It was neat. We saw litanig clouds. It was sunny. It was hot at the time. My sister sings like rock stars. We saw a lot of fly's. It was very, very, very neat.

(Bronwyn) I love it here. I wish I cold live here. I'm eight. My mom works for Compterservis.

(Laura) I brought my ghetto-blaster and we could get almost every station. We even got a station from Medford and a couple TV stations too. The sunset was totally awesome. The fog has been moving up and it looks like the sea is overflowing. It's really cool. We brought our dog, Corky, and he likes it too.

(Mary) At first I was apprehensive about bringing the girls up here to spend the night, but after reading what they wrote, I know they really enjoyed themselves.

August 17, 18 and 19 - Rick and Robbie C.; North Bend, OR

(Robbie) There is an unusual cleansing feeling you get from these mountains. We have found a place where we can truly forget the everyday mundane worries of work and other troubles.

After three days, we're still not tired of the views, wish we had three more.

Dave and Karran H. met us here the first day. We played hard. I go home with some cuts, bruises and a lump on my head when I fell down. Champagne will do that sometimes.

We spent several hours trying to find Snow Camp Meadow. Dave was convinced the markings on the ground in the meadow were from an alien spacecraft.

The first night we grilled some big steaks and played poker. I beat the pants off everyone and when I went outside to get some ice, they stole my chips. Cheaters!

Dave and Karran left the afternoon of the second day. Their departure gave Rick and I some peace and quiet and some time alone. This has been one of the best times of our lives. We are already planning our next trip to Snow Camp Lookout. Thanks to the U.S. Forest Service for sharing this treasure with the public.

August 19, 20 and 21 - Jim and Kimber G.; Eugene, OR

Be sure to go north to the rocky edge of this summit. Great view of meadow and alien drawing.

August 21, 22 and 23 - John and Chad T.; Monmouth, OR

We left our house around 8:15 A.M. and arrived at the lookout around 4:30 P.M. We got lost on our way up here on these dang logging roads. We saw a lot of lizards and a mouse! We saw an unusual alien drawing down in Snow Camp Meadow.

(August 22) After lunch, we hiked the roads to Fairview Meadows. There we met a fellow who was setting up camp for a group of bear hunters who use bows. They will hang a fish in between two trees as bait. The bears come into the camp after the bait. He assured us they got bear each year.

Last night, I awoke to the noise of papers rustling. After being unable to return to sleep, I caught sight of something moving on the floor. I shined the flashlight and found a mouse scampering around. After moving the food out of the lower cupboard, he gave up and returned to his home in the woodbox. We awoke this A.M. to find he had chewed his way into our loaf of strawberry bread.

August 24 - John and Connie H.; Coos Bay, OR.

The alien design in Snow Camp Meadow seems to have been made by a gas powered weed eater.

August 27, 28, 29, 30 and 31 - David L. and Inez C.; Crescent City, CA

We arrived about five last night, the day after our wedding. Had to let the pickup cool for an hour at the fork with road #550, so we sat in the road and played cribbage in the dirt. Most of our stuff is still at the bottom of the hill, where much of it will remain. The Forest Service has given the word "strenuous" a new meaning.

Such a joy to find coffee (with a note from former campers), condiments, the lovely painting and all that wood. It feels like coming home at a time when we're exhausted and stressed out. We'll have five days here to recoup our strength, recover from months of children, grandchildren, preparations. We did manage to drag our sparkling apple cider and the "bride and groom" crystal goblets up the hill. Sat here and watched the moon come up and toasted our marriage by moonlight. After living together for nine years, we have no major adjustments to make, but I'm amazed at how putting this wedding together has deepened commitment, magnified tenderness. This is the best place in the world for a honeymoon.

This morning, we watch clouds form, fog sneak into low spots like a child slipping silently away from Saturday morning chores. One more laborious trip to and from the pickup, then a breakfast that would fill three men and a large dog, but left us licking our plates. Socked in, our little ridge an island.

(August 28) It began to storm at noon yesterday and no sign of letup yet. Gusting high winds, rain pounding against the south and west windows. We put a flat dishpan outside (held down with a six pack of Pepsi), and according to this rain gauge, we've had two and a half inches of rain. *Every* south window leaks!! We tried to staunch the flow into the bed with all our towels, but it was like trying to keep slugs out of the peas by throwing them (slugs) over the fence—an exercise in futility. So we gracefully accepted the inevitable and had a lovely, romantic evening with candles, music and the last of the cider.

This morning about 10 A.M. the room was suddenly full of boiling smoke from the stove. Opened the east window and the door; smoke billowed from the stove's cracks, dampers, joints in the pipe. We know the rules say don't empty the stove but we moved the stove's contents to the gravel and doused it with water. When we held a lighted match inside, the chimney didn't draw at all. We're supposed to be here until Saturday, and the truck would never make it up that hill when the road's wet, so going to the ranger station is out. Somehow, we either have to fix it ourselves, stay cold, or go home. Poor dog is begging to go home, but we'll sit tight tonight and maybe the storm will be over in the morning.

Between us, we've lived on this coast almost 100 years. David figures winds at 20 to 30 mph, gusts to 40. I figure about five mph higher. Temperature is about fifty degrees inside.

What an incredible experience!! Last night, it got *very* cold in here, and we've upped our estimate of the wind velocity considerably. We had sustained wind out of the southwest at about 40, with gusts to 65. This wonderful old building seemed to crouch and brace itself. Sabbath, our beloved Bull Terrier, is afraid of wind, and she was cold, homesick and confused. We put her in bed with us and the three of us rode out the night in a group snuggle. Plan to spend the day in bed, drinking coffee, eating and reading aloud *The Tao of Pooh*.

We've a little Coleman stove, and while we were making coffee and scrambled eggs, a Curry County sheriff's deputy suddenly appeared on the balcony. Came to check on how we were riding out the storm, which goes on and on. He passed up breakfast, but said he'd let the Forest Service know we have no heat. We also have zero visibility, we literally didn't see him coming. It looks as though our honeymoon, like our wedding, will be unique.

The whole south side of the building is wet, with water flowing unimpeded through the window frames. The temperature inside is the same as outside but the wind velocity is a little lower. Sabbath still has her nose tucked into the covers, hoping we won't see her and throw her out.

(4 P.M.) Back to bed this morning for a read and a warm nap. Woke just as help arrived about 2:30. A beautiful man in a blue pickup truck and a ladder! Spent ten minutes on the roof and came down with a screen filled with creosote, and apologies all over his head and face. Seems the Forest Service asked him to put in the screen when the fire danger was high. We've praised and encouraged the beautiful little stove and it's beginning to warm up in here.

(August 30) SUNSHINE! Woke to stars, moonlight and last of the clouds blowing away. It's Friday; we have been socked in with a maximum of 100 feet of visibility since noon Tuesday. So glad that our last day here (we leave at noon tomorrow), will provide us with the views we've read about in this journal. It's been like living in *The Neverending Story*.

(August 31) Thanks to the FS and the wheelbarrow they left and the one we brought from home, the pack in and out is much easier.

September 1 and 2 - Beth, Jeff, Nate and Nellie B.; Grants Pass, OR

Very happy to let the 4-runner climb "the hill" to ease our unloading. Thanks for the wood, water and supplies. We hauled a round of Douglas fir to the top and would have been sunk without more wood when our Coleman went on the fritz just when I had the chili makings ready to cook. Vegetarian chili and brown rice pilaf on the wood stove worked fine.

Bushwhacked down an old trail to Snow Camp Meadow, then returned via the road, a five mile trip? The seven and eleven year olds came through like champs once we started singing.

The house mouse paid a visit. The kids found his pink ears cute.

(August 2, 2:17 P.M.) Lunching after return from Windy Valley. A four hour hike. Our estimate is 2.5 very steep miles with loose rocks, rocky trail bed, muddy spots. Not for the fainthearted hiker. The reward is great old growth cedar, lush meadow grass, darlingtonia bogs and a clear mountain stream. For some reason, it seemed shorter coming back...we knew where we were going. The misleading distance on the sign leaves the unwary hiker wondering who's crazy; in this case, the USFS certainly is. One and one-half miles by air, at least one mile further on foot.

Lookout rental is a great idea. Snow Camp is very comfortable. We're going to suggest a similar effort be made at Hersberger Lookout in the Rogue River National Forest, a few miles from Crater Lake, and Rabbit Ears at the Rogue-Umpqua Divide Wilderness. All in favor—send letters to the supervisor of the Rogue River National Forest.

September 3 - Michael, Caren, Sarah, Charles and Hannah L.; Eugene, OR

This is written one year later, because we didn't make it last year, though we did get close. Loaded the van up in Eugene for the family's first outdoor adventure, the family being parents plus a five year old (Sarah), two year old (Charles), and four month old (Hannah). The key to get into the lookout had not arrived in the mail, as the USFS promised...but, by phone they assured it would be waiting in the mailbox at the ranger station (it was the weekend). With that promise (you've got to believe Uncle Sam and Smokey the Bear), we loaded the car with all the baby paraphernalia and camping equipment and took off in a driving rainstorm, certain it would be beautiful once we hit the coast...it only got worse. We just knew it would be better going south...and we were wrong. Something should have told us right there to give up and go home, but we kept on driving to Gold Beach.

We got to Gold Beach mid afternoon, went to the ranger station, but no key. We discussed (very rationally and calmly...sort of), the various options, and decided driving up here without the key was not the best option. Second choice, call every Reilley in the phone book to get hold of the person I'd made the reservation with. I talked with so many Reilleys with so many different spellings. No help and they must have thought I was crazy. The children at this point are crying, very loud, the rain is so heavy you can't see through the windshield and my husband, Michael, is staring straight ahead, not saying a word. There is no hotel space anywhere and we are facing the long drive back to Eugene with three crying and tired children, two of whom want to go camping and can't figure out why we're going home. But home we went, in the rain. The clouds broke up and the sun came out around Humbug Mountain—no more rain all the way home.

The final outcome: Two nights free at the lookout the following year with our choice of days and more important, combination locks instead of keys. (See the continuing saga of our family on August 8 and 9, 1992.)

September 8 - Peggy and James V.; Hebo, OR

Nice stay here this weekend, but too short! Being on lookout was a sentimental journey for us, as a former smokejumper and a former lookout. Can't say we missed the radio though! It's certainly more peaceful without the constant FS chatter and the need to do a scan for smokes every fifteen minutes. We're looking forward to finding out more about the lookout rental program, both here in Oregon and elsewhere. I hope it will be a success and inspire the Forest Service to preserve as many lookouts as possible instead of allowing them to fall into disrepair and then destroying them.

September 9, 10 and 11 - Lisa I. and Robert V.; Bend, OR

The Rogue River boat trip out of Gold Beach was excellent! Then we went to Brookings, bought some kites and hit the beach. This place is great. Good night.

That was the last entry for Snow Camp's 1991 season.

LOOKOUT INFORMATION

For the uninitiated, the term "lookout" has a dual definition. It refers to the person who looks for forest fires and the buildings and towers that they lived in.

Around 1953, America had as many as 5,060 lookouts spread across the nation. Oregon had 805 and Idaho had the most with 966. At first lookouts were simple camps on a high ridge or mountaintop. Some of the earliest lookouts, beginning around 1910, were just platforms in a treetop with slats nailed to the tree to serve as a ladder. These eventually evolved from tree houses with ground tents to permanent glass houses. They stood on high points in the forest nearly everywhere. It was America's assault on forest fires, a crucial first line of defense, the early warning system. During the 1950s and 60s, lookouts were being phased out due to the use of airplanes. Today there are only a few hundred lookouts being actively staffed across the country.

At first, a lookout had only his sharp eyes and perhaps a pair of binoculars to spot fires. When he did spot a fire, he sometimes went out by himself to put it out if possible. Later, sophisticated Osborne Firefinders became standard equipment along with telephones and radios to report a fire to a central dispatcher who then sent a crew to fight the blaze.

Lookouts were usually manned during the summer months. The fire lookout was constantly vigilant for smoke. Once smoke was seen, the lookout tried to determine if it was an actual fire, or maybe just dust, fog or clouds, which can look like smoke from a distance. An Osborne Firefinder was used to pinpoint the smoke on a map. A lookout had to be familiar with the surrounding terrain. When he reported to the dispatcher, he was usually able to give information about the fire such as exact location, estimated size, the type of vegetation it was in, wind direction/speed and color/character of the smoke. Once the dispatcher received the initial call, the smoke often could be cross-checked and precisely pinpointed by other lookouts.

The Osborne Firefinder was first introduced about 1915. An improved model in 1934 was mounted in thousands of lookouts. It was similar in principle to a surveyor's transit and usually located in the center of the lookout on a sliding base that allowed the lookout to see around obstacles such as window frames. Mounted beneath the instrument was a map of the "seen" area. A sighting of smoke could be plotted with amazing accuracy by using a front peep sight and rear cross hairs (or a spotting scope on the later models). Those familiar with the firefinder could pinpoint a smoke across miles of terrain to within a few hundred feet.

To be a lookout took a special person, someone comfortable with the outdoors and with their own thoughts, able to respect and weather nature's fury. Fire lookouts are frequently buffeted by fierce storms and sometimes struck by lightning. They were protected by an elaborate system of grounding wires. Nonetheless, being in a lookout during a lightning storm is an unnerving experience. Each lookout would be equipped with a chair or stool with glass insulators on its legs to give the one manning the tower a "safe" place to sit when the lightning storm was close.

Lookouts tell about storms raining yellowish green sparks, or of bluish fireballs flashing around the walkway and sometimes coming inside and leaping from the stove to the radio.

There was also a long list of instructions as to their duties during a lightning storm such as plotting lightning strikes, and things not to do (like touching the stove or telephone). The distance from the lookout to the point of a strike could be calculated roughly by counting the number of seconds between a flash and the report of thunder following, (about 1,100 feet per second or one mile for each five seconds).

At Calimus Butte, in south central Oregon, the lookout cabin is located on a pyrite deposit. Six lookouts have been knocked unconscious by lightning while inside the cabin and a seventh person was in the outhouse when it was hit. On Strawberry Mountain in southwest Washington, the Brown brothers were repairing telephone line when the portable telephone began ringing faintly. Just as brother Carroll reached to answer it, lightning struck, knocking him unconscious. He survived the ordeal; however, the woodpile was reduced to ashes.

Even though a lookout was somewhat on his or her own, there was a long list of duties for them to accomplish. The Forest Service handbook outlined the following:

1. Keep all windows clean inside and out at all times.
2. Insure that the cabin interior and exterior grounds are clean and sanitary.
3. Be accurate, neat and orderly in maintaining the daily logbook.
4. Each time you leave the tower, let the dispatcher know when you leave, where you're going and when you plan to return.
5. Learn every peak, ridge, hill, road, trail, lake, creek, building and false smoke. Be able to plot their legal description to the nearest 40-corner.
6. Know how to use the map, compass, protractor, Pulaski, Lookout Cookbook, fuel moisture sticks, wet bulb thermometer, rain gauge anemometer, fan psychrometer, hygrothermograph and Osborne firefinder.
7. Check lightning protection system immediately upon arriving at the station and again after each storm.
8. Be able to pace the progress of a thunderstorm before it arrives overhead.
9. Make a systematic and complete scan of the visible area, using no less than twenty minutes out of every hour every day.
10. Know how to gauge the progress of a fire's behavior by the smoke column. Be able to calculate its acreage with the firefinder vernier scale.
11. Be able to make necessary repairs on the telephone and phone line.
12. Maintain a 48 hour fresh water supply and a ten day supply of choped wood at all times.
13. Have the Fireman's pack complete and ready to go and keep yourself physically prepared for long and continuous duty at a fire.

Finally, a quote from the Forest Service chief: "Guard against becoming impatient with the general public. For some of them, you will be their first contact with the Forest Service. Answer their questions with integrity and enthusiasm. Remember, you are the representative of a very important organization. Don't let it down."

A lookout's job could be very boring and lonely. Days would turn into weeks and sometimes months with no visits by another human. When he or she did have a visitor, it was just as likely to be a supervisor to conduct an inspection. A new lookout was especially prone to the loneliness, and many never made it through their first summer.

When a young lady at Cleman Lookout near Naches, Washington, felt she couldn't take it anymore, she found herself crying to the dispatcher on the radio, "I quit. Come and get me out of here!" But the next person wasn't her replacement, it was the game warden with a newly orphaned elk calf for her to take care of.

Suddenly Linda's schedule was very busy with the duties every mother is familiar with. Eight bottle feedings a day and she forgot all about wanting to quit. The calf grew rapidly and became a frisky young bull. His playing would include pawing the ground, snorting as he threw his head back and then running to her when she whistled. Every day they would take long walks together. By summer's end, their bond was complete. As Linda said "good-bye" to her nearly full grown friend and reluctantly left the mountain, she began making plans for her next season at Cleman Lookout.

Many lookouts were "manned" by women. One of the first lookouts in America was Mabel Gray in 1902, who between cooking for a logging camp, hiked twice a day to the top of Bertha Hill near Headquarters, Idaho, to check for smokes. Hallie Daggett went to work at Eddy Gulch Lookout in Siskiyou County, California and became known from coast to coast. During her fifteen year career she was featured in a number of newspapers, creating a flood of applications by young women for lookout jobs with the Forest Service.

Courtships have even been carried on via the two-way radio from lookout to lookout, sometimes with a person they didn't see until the end of summer. One man just had to meet that lady lookout whom he'd been hearing on the radio. He left one morning and took a long walk from his lookout to hers. Just as he arrived there, the telephone rang, but it was **his** ring...two longs and four shorts. Pretending to be at his lookout, he answered it and just as he thought he was going to get away with his deception, the boss told him to step outside and count the number of boards on the catwalk. Calling back a few minutes later, he told the ranger the count was thirty. The reply was, "Wrong, son, there is forty at your lookout. Now get yourself back to your own mountain...pronto!"

Building plans for lookouts became standardized about 1915. The first was the D-6 Cupola. It was a 12' X 12' frame house with windows all around. What made it distinctive was a glassed-in, centered, second story cupola with about one-fourth the floor space of the first floor and used for observation.

The L-4 came into existence about 1930. It measured 14' X 14' and had a gabled roof with heavy shutters that were hinged above the windows. These were propped open in the summer months to shade the windows, and securely fastened shut during winter months.

The L-4 Aladdin (built between 1933 and 1953), was named after its manufacturer, the Aladdin Company. These had a hip roof and were precut mail-order bungalows. The cost was $500 FOB Spokane or Portland.

The L-5 was similar to the L-4 except it measured 10' X 10'.

The L-6 cab measured only 8' X 8' and was typically mounted on an 80 to 100 foot tower.

The R-6 Flattop was first constructed in 1953 and became the Forest Service standard. It measures 14' X 14' and has a large flat roof. Snow Camp Lookout is an R-6.

Some were elevated on steel towers; the tallest was 123 feet on Moses Mountain in Washington's Colville Indian Reservation. One of the most ingenious lookouts was the Cook Creek spar tree on the Quinault Indian Reservation that gained national recognition in the late 1920s. Imagine a massive fir tree that is 179 feet tall after being "topped" and its limbs removed. A 7' X 7' building perched around the tree's top, and a spiral "staircase" wound around the tree from top to bottom. The staircase consisted of 130 three foot long steel bolts with an eye in the end. These were driven into the tree and held securely with a cable run through each eye and stretched tight. The very top of the tree protruded into the little building and the firefinder sat on the top. The spar tree was securely fastened with guy wires to keep it steady in a wind.

The world's two tallest lookouts are the Warren Bicentennial Tree Lookout at 225.7 feet and the Gloucester Tree at 200.1 feet, both located in Western Australia. These are actually metal cabs mounted in towering eucalyptus trees in the Karri Forest 310 km south of Perth, near Pemberton. This was simply the easiest way to watch for fire in a flat landscape covered by very tall trees.

Many lookouts were named after wildlife such as: Rattlesnake, Grizzly, Coyote, Eagle, Bear, Wolf, Grasshopper, Elephant, Jackass, Lynx, Goat, Crane, Yellowjacket, Mule, Raven, Sheep, Fox, Panther and Horse. A host of lookouts were given Indian names and every forest seemed to have at least one called "Lookout Mountain." A sampling of others would be: Muck-a-Muck, Postage Stamp, Skull and Crossbones, Gunsight, High Heaven, Devil's Backbone, Foul

**LOOKING SOUTH OVER THE TOP
OF THE OLD OUTHOUSE TOWARD BROOKINGS**

"SOLAR SHOWER VIEW"

Weather, Gobbler's Knob, Thunder Mountain, Rooster Rock, Desolation, Fuzztail, Dirtyface and Hump Tulips.

Today, few lookouts remain compared to their numbers four decades ago. Over the years these lofty buildings have bowed to the advancements of technology. Lookouts have been replaced with a better network of roads, cellular telephones, airplanes and helicopters. Many of the aircraft are also equipped with infrared sensors to pick up sources of heat below.

Perhaps the day will come when remote-controlled, heat-sensing devices mounted on mountaintops will scan the countryside. A dispatcher in control center many miles away will detect a fire, plot its exact coordinates and send a fire fighting team…all from the same chair. Will we someday use sentinel satellites in space to signal a fire's presence?

Lookouts were once the eyes of the Forest Service and though their heyday has passed, let us hope we can preserve those that remain for future generations to know, enjoy and experience!

SNOW CAMP JOURNAL — 1992

May 29 - Kathleen, Elizabeth, Daniel, Marc and Caitlin Anne O.

(Elizabeth, age 9) It is beautiful. It is very hard to get up the hill and we had the whole back of a large four door station wagon stuffed and things in the front.

All the scribbles are from Caitlin Anne, almost nineteen months old. She says "Hi Hi." My mom, Kathleen, likes it because she likes being away from electricity and phones. I just love this place. I don't like the door knob that keeps sticking.

In the evening it is very windy. The wind pushed us when we stood up. It knocked things down and messed up our hair when Daddy took our pictures.

We went on the Windy Valley trail and the kids (Daniel, Marc and Elizabeth), ran ahead. When Dad found out it was three miles long, we were long ahead. Dad called and called to us and we heard him *once*. We thought that Dad or someone was hurt and it was about one-fourth of a mile back uphill. Well, no one was hurt. They just wanted to get us back. I was scared to death that they were hurt. We found them sitting and Caitlin was crying. BUT, it was just because she was mad at Mom. Everyone was OK. I was crying really hard. But then we got to go to the mine. It is on the walk up path. If you look toward the side where it goes off into the valley. One side is under the dirt. Not really a mine. I said to myself, I want to sleep in here, but I did not. We had much more advenchures but no more boom!

If we come again, I'll try to tell you the rest. Probably not. Don't expect it. Caitlin says, "By by guy!" Cool.

(Kathleen) I have read the Laura Ingalls Wilder books and it is like living here. Like Laura, we cooked dinner on the wood burning stove.

June 11 and 12 - Maya R.; Williams, OR

I am having a baby in two days so I am very full and this rest is wonderful and likewise the rain...the blessed rain falling to the dry Mother Earth. My mind has had a chance to flow out of its boxes of everyday small thoughts and this is good.

We will be back September 20 and 21 with our baby for our anniversary and my husband's birthday. I really enjoy the journal, full of the history of this country. I will bring some reading material to leave here in this special retreat space.

I drank out of "Timothy's" mouse cup before I read about it in the journal. I am praying for good health.

June 13 and 14 - Lyndell, Wendy, Jim and Jane; Eugene, OR

(Wendy) We came all the way down here and we can only see the solar powered outhouse. We have absolutely no view. The fog is so thick, we just about need a guide dog to take us up the road. We tried to take a nature walk but it was cut short due to the rain. Only one of us was smart enough to bring rain gear and a hat.

(June 14, 7 A.M.) We all prayed to the "Clearing Gods" and we did a "Clearing Dance" and lo, we awoke to beautiful, green peaks and valleys, buttes and trails, the ocean and the clouds and even a cluster of buildings in the distance.

(4:45 P.M.) We're still alive 24 hours after we arrived. Once again, the fog has returned to haunt us or perhaps just tease us. We had a nice walk this morning, but were forced back early around 1 P.M. due to rain again. Thus, Jane and Wendy were reduced to a nap and Lyndell tried to show Jim how to read a compass. It doesn't matter anyway, we can't see the "true north" from the south, nor the east from the west.

However, we still know, with the aid of the compass, as Jim has informed me, which direction is which.

(Monday, 7:04 A.M.) After being forced to get up before the official "get up" time of 6:30 A.M., once again I find myself writing. Last night, after a lovely dinner of spaghetti and fettucine/tuna mix, we found ourselves socked in by fog for the last time. At approximately 10:30 P.M., Lyndell discovered a break in the fog. Thus, Wendy and Lyndell were able to successfully view a lunar eclipse, which lasted to approximately 11:30 P.M. With binoculars, we were able to observe craters, volcanoes and mountains of the moon — very spectacular! We viewed this among the sounds of the wind through the wood stove and whistling snores of Jim. There was romance to it...Lyndell and I agreed it was the best view we had ever had of the moon.

In speculation, I think we all enjoyed ourselves. Jane says, "It could have been a little bit better." Lyndell says, "It was fine; we got some wails in." Jim says, "It was very beneficial and would like to come back when the damn weather would be good." And I say, "I enjoyed myself and the company I was with and I say we make this an annual retreat."

44

I leave you with words of wisdom. Life is short, so do all you can. Go for it! Take a chance!

By the way, watch out for ants!

June 19, 20 and 21 - Derek G. and Julia S.; Brookings, OR

What a haul up the hill! Took us three trips each to get everything up. Good exercise, I kept saying.

No sleeping in at this place. Nothing like having the sun shine right in your eyes.

ANTS! Have faith, Derek took the can of "Drop Dead" and got 90+% of them. We believe their farm is below the *"Pack It Home"* poster outside. We never had any more problems with them.

What a nice hike to Windy Valley. We stumbled upon a herd of elk in the first mile. It was quite a shock. They were surprised to see us and we were surprised to see them, to say the least. We had forgotten how big elk are.

Lots of pretty flowers, plants and scenery on the way down. We walked up the creek and sat on a big log that crosses the creek. Very pretty and surreal. Well worth the effort to get there.

June 24 - Ginny and Bill S. (and two boys); Salem, OR

Elk! Twenty-five in the meadow this evening. Even saw two fawns. Nice day, good weather.

Windy Creek trail is not well marked. Beware the white ribbons, they go on forever and you never get to the creek that way.

I swore I wouldn't go on another long hike after yesterday's but that was yesterday. We decided to go down to Snow Camp Meadow to see if it was as beautiful from down there. We went over the side by the car park, hoping to find a trail. We ended up blazing our own through the bushes, etc. It wasn't easy but about one hour later we reached the bottom. We didn't see the elk today but this is one of their main hangouts.

We found a trail up, wound around and ended up back on that blasted Windy Creek trail, taking about two hours altogether coming back. The trails are not well marked.

Our only problem has been water. We couldn't carry enough for the entire stay in our Vega which also really cried coming up the last two miles of hill. Instead of taking the car out again and taking the chance that it wouldn't make it back, the boys carried in water from Windy Creek yesterday and some from a running stream we found on our walk to the meadow. That wasn't easy. We purified it and I think we now have plenty.

We saw some little birds, one little yellow one that was very curious and sat six inches from us. One almost landed on Bill's finger. Also saw some beautiful pinkish-white flowers that smelled like the perfume shop in Disneyland.

It is very peaceful and beautiful here. We haven't seen a soul since we've been here. Very glad we came.

July 1 and 2 - Ed, Kelly and Marva; Medford, OR

(Marva) This is one teenager *not* into the great outdoors like her parents.

We've been most fortunate to be able to see almost every type of perfect view mentioned in the journal. We've had perfect weather. No bugs, flies or mice. Wildlife reviewed included many elk, deer (one huge buck with a rack already ten inches above ears), a spotted owl (up very close), a mother quail with a dozen fluffy chicks, lizards, chipmunks and birds.

I'm thankful for this wonderful time.

July 4 - Ted, Barbara and Megan S.

We enjoyed the chipmunk family who stuffed their cheeks with shelled peanuts, then squirreled their bounty in hidden places. Be careful on the woodpile, they often scurry around under the wood! We sure appreciate this retreat. Thanks to the volunteers and fellow campers who created and maintain this haven.

July 6 and 7 - Henry and Mary S.

The senior S.'s followed our children.

Those dear little chipmunks we view with some reservation. They are quite bold and come in open windows to chew on paper-wrapped food. Anyway, we fed (left them), piles of crackers on the picnic table hoping they overeat and stay outside tonight.

We have really enjoyed our two days here. The weather was perfect and the scenery unsurpassed. We went on three hikes and saw five deer. The Forest Service is to be commended for providing such a facility to the public.

July 9 and 10 - Linda and Amy B. and Benjamin K.; Crescent City, CA

(Linda) We left home about 10:30 A.M. Stopped at Nook Bar and swam. Headed up to Snow Camp about 3:30 P.M. Stopped at Humboldt Creek to let the truck cool off. Pulled up to the gate and my front tire goes flat. But I came prepared. Dig out can of tire fix-it, fill tire. The problem is that fix-it won't work if there is a slit on the inside wall of the tire that you could put your finger in. But I'm still prepared! Dig out jack, raise front end, go back for spare. Thankfully, I have my sixteen year old nephew to do the crawling under the rig. But he can't get the spare down because the bolt is rusted that holds it up. We are still on the wrong side of the gate! Next, we dig out our portable air compressor. I figure that I will try to get enough air in the tire to make it to the parking lot. We load everything back in the truck while Ben is filling the tire with air. Soon as it is up we make a beeline for the parking lot. Ben is hanging out the window to watch the air level in the tire. (The tire is already ruined but I want to save the rim.) With a few prayers, we made it.

We give up on the truck. We just have enough energy to climb the hill. Thank you for the wheelbarrow. It is a strange feeling to be out this far without transportation.

The worst part is that my family is not looking for us to be home until Sunday, late. We only have two nights here at the lookout, then we were going to camp on the river Saturday.

(9 P.M.) The wind is really blowing. The sky is clear. Amy and Ben are having fun. The moon is up and it is bright outside. Amy is making hand shadow puppets by moonlight.

(3 A.M.) The moon has set now. We are surrounded by stars. Wind is still shaking the building.

(7:30 A.M.) Rise and shine. After breakfast, we are going down to tackle the tire. Wind still blowing.

(10:30 A.M.) We made it! After putting the jack under the spare, we were able to break the bolt loose. We now have transportation but I am afraid of exploring without a spare so we will be hanging around here today. Amy has brought me butterflies and lizards. We spotted a barge off shore, headed north.

(1 P.M.) Wind has stopped blowing, eighty degrees in the shade. Kids are still collecting insects. While reading some of the articles, I have learned that we are thirteen air miles from the ocean.

(6 P.M.) Wind is blowing so hard, it is a real thrill just getting to the bathroom and back.

July 11, 12 and 13 - Dave K. and Kim P.; Eugene, OR

After reading entries in the journal, we realized we were taking our gorgeous day for granted. The weather was beautiful with only a light breeze. On the way in, just outside Gold Beach, Dave began telling me how much water is used nationwide by restaurants. Just about the time we hit the gravel road, I realized, "water!" We forgot our water. So, back to town for water. In the meantime, we discovered we'd forgotten the lid to our water jug too.

Luckily, we made it back to town before the stores closed and we were able to find another jug and a lid (off a large spice jar), which fit our original water jug. Needless to say, we got up to the lookout later than originally anticipated. Just natural for us. Anyway, view was beautiful, weather great, sunset gorgeous. And, thanks to a mouse rummaging through our food sacks, we were given the opportunity to watch the moon set — beautiful orange, sinking beneath the clouds on the horizon. Earlier, we missed the sun fall beneath the sky, as I was chopping wood. Turned around and the sun was gone. The sky was beautiful!

Plan to hike to Fairview Meadow today. Decided we should…seems like everyone else has. Would hate to end a tradition.

Decided to take our raft and drive to Panther Lake. Drove for about one hour only to find out that the lake is now a swampy marsh. Figured we would try to find the lake you can see from the lookout; be advised it's about the size of a small swimming pool and the water has a very unappetizing look, once you are right on top of it. Strike two.

Decided to drive to town, gas up and go to the Rogue. Got gas but figured that there would probably be about one million people on the Rogue so we went to the Pistol River instead. Drove around for awhile before we could find a place to get down to the river with the raft (it's a six man raft and we didn't want to carry it too far). Found a spot, got down and had a great time. The water is clean and warm and there are some very nice swimming holes.

On the trip back up, we decided to walk into Fairview Meadow. Once again, keeping up with tradition, we too were unable to find it.

When we got back to the lookout, we noticed someone had been to the top before us (i.e., someone had used the john). Figured it was the Forest Service checking on things.

Later that night, when we had another visitor around 11 P.M., we began to think otherwise. Our visitor made himself known by driving to the *top* of the hill, turning around out front and exiting. Nothing was bothered, checked the car and bikes in the morning, but sure scared the hell out of me. What somebody was doing up here at 11 P.M., and that somebody knew the combination to the lock, caught our attention to say the least.

We made up all kinds of scenarios, the most logical (we hoped), was that the person wanted to see if anybody was here; then, rather than look sneaky, went ahead and drove to the top to let the occupants know he wasn't after anything. Oh well, got me through the night. We decided next time we'd bring our own combination lock and use it. The Forest Service has keys to the other lock on the gate so it won't keep any legitimate visitors away.

Well, we're leaving this haven. We had a great time, beautiful and all around great experience. Had hoped to see a thunder and lightning storm from up here, but that's O.K., couldn't have had better weather. Still no wind. We're off now for the rest of our vacation, Moab, Utah, to do some "heavy" mountain bike riding.

July 13, 14 and 15 - Lensay M. and Kert K.; Knoxville and Nashville, TN.

They need things like this back in Tennessee.

July 17 - Mae, Emily and Sarah N.; Albany, OR.

(Mae, age 12) We finally got here! First we thought we were lost but we got here! We had a nice time, calm winds and warm weather. We saw some moths, lizards and lots of bugs. We also saw deer and birds. We didn't hear the mouse but I had to call it something so I called it "Sam the Second" after my cat at home. I love this place! (Sorry I wrote so bad, I just woke up!)

(Emily, age 9) It's wonderful here! I guess it was worth it to drive all the way up here! One thing I don't like about this place is the bathroom. It's too hard getting there, back and forth, and it smells in there too! But everything else is neat! It's really a cool place. I LOVE IT! I wish there were horses here so we could ride.

July 17 - Unknown author

Two of the unexpected joys were: The outhouse—leaving the door propped open afforded the most magnificent view a "throne room" ever experienced! The second was in reading these journals. How wonderful to hear of the histories and how far people came to enjoy this mountain paradise.

July 17, 18 and 19 - Roger, Donna, B.J. and Danny S.; Gig Harbor, WA

(Roger) We arrived about 3:30, July 17. We spent two days here last year and were excited to spend another couple of days. Unfortunately the camp people sent us the wrong combination. My wife, who should probably take up safe cracking, had two of the numbers figured out before a Forest Service truck came by and radioed in for the correct combinations.

We were also treated to a passing thunder storm. We saw lots of lightning while we ate breakfast.

(Donna) It is always a treat to go camping but this is really something. A comfortable place to stay in the middle of what feels like nowhere, with an incredible view and it's always different. Always! Of course, we've only been here twice! We enjoyed incredible weather, saw deer and a blue heron down below by the river, chipmunks and "Timothy" mouse.

July 21 and 22 - Dave and Peggy L.; Rogue River, OR (Home of the National Rooster Crowing Contest)

Our day started off on the wrong foot. We were sent the wrong combination! But as we traveled back down the mountain, we ran into a Forest Service employee who radioed for the combination and followed us back to the lookout to make sure it worked. He is our hero! He even brought our gear up to the lookout door. Thank you bunches, kind sir.

The night was quiet until 3 A.M. I awoke to something in the wood bin I roused my husband who sat up, laid down and went back to sleep. I stood guard through the next hour just in case our visitor decided to visit our side of the room. I was afraid he could smell the chocolate chip cookies that we had eaten in bed. Visions of little feet running across my nose kept me alert.

As I write in the journal, David is busy packing. Maybe if I look busy enough, he'll have it all done by the time I'm finished writing. Still foggy.

This was my birthday gift to my husband for his thirty-seventh birthday yesterday. We've enjoyed our time so much that we plan on stopping in town to reserve a weekend next year. Maybe we'll bring our daughters... maybe.

July 24 - The R. Family; Columbus, OH

Arrived at noon. Where are the Sherpas? Winds steadily from the east and very noisy. Beautiful sounds created by the wind and keeps the flying insects away. Where are the creatures who eat flying insects anyway?

The most stunning crescent moon ever. It was so clear, you could see the features on the dark side of the moon opposite the crescent. Slept on the porch, too warm for down sleeping bag. I fell asleep staring at the Milky Way with my mouth open.

Hummingbird enters, attracted to red fire extinguishers. This place lacks for nothing. The wind is especially welcome, having cleaned out some debris from between my ears. People who have been here before me have left a vivid impression of proprietorship and good house keeping. Selfishly, I would not like word of this to get out and attract the subhuman type of people here who find their thrills in vandalism. I'll never go to a crowded campground again.

Thanks for the wheelbarrow.

July 25, 26 and 27 - Rick and Robbie C.; North Bend, OR

Our second of what we hope to be many years at Snow Camp. There are no words to describe the feelings we get from this experience. We can only thank the U.S. Forest Service for sharing this treasure and hope they continue.

July 28 - Clint W. and Grandpa; West Covina, CA

I couldn't wait until the stars started coming out. When they finally did, I was astonished. I had never seen so many stars, even shooting ones.

When we went to bed, I told grandpa to sleep in the bed and I'll sack up on the floor which was a mistake. I had just gone into "la la land" when I felt something cold on my hand (which was moving). I woke up and it was a mouse. I knocked him off and tried to go back to sleep but many more mice came out which angered me. This also makes you feel at one with nature, so that's why I slept on the countertop on the south side of the lookout.

With the sun as your alarm clock, you will definitely wake up early. I did. It's neat how the fog sits in the valleys where the rivers are. It's so peaceful up here. I could live like this, minus the mice.

Oh yeah, when using the rest room, leave the door open and you can breath much better and you have a nice view.

Death makes angels of us all,

And gives us wings where we had shoulders,

Smooth as ravens claws.

Up here in the perimeter there are many stars,

Up here we is stoned immaculate.

Aware, shake dreams from your hair my pretty child, my sweet one.

Choose the day, choose the sign of your day, the day diminishes.

First thing you see, vast radiant beach, cool jeweled moon, awake.

August 1 - Bonnie and Mike D.; Coos Bay, OR via FL, OH and PA

What a magical place! It is so peaceful at this lookout that somehow it seems like I've died and gone to heaven.

The first sight of Snow Camp, I somehow knew that I would enjoy my visit, but the trip up the "hill" was a little much. Maybe steps would be a good idea, naw...the hike is worth the beauty. You have to work hard for great things.

Saw boats on the ocean, got sunburned, read the journal and awaited the critters' arrival. The bees and flies showed up first. It sounds like a "small insect airport" up here and we are the "bee traffic controllers."

It is going to be hard going back into civilization (or is it?). Oh...the philosophy sessions we could get into on that question.

51

I was surprised not to see more birds here. I guess being up 4,000 feet, we surpass the food chain known to our feathered friends.

First the chipmunks came for caramel popcorn, then the sunset. A flaming ball of fire settling in for the evening, falling into the foam layer on the edge of the earth. I can almost hear it sizzle as it hits the ocean. Just gorgeous!

As Arnold Schwarzenegger would say, "We'll be back!"

August 2, 3, 4 and 5 - Gloria and John S.; Gold Beach, OR

We have done nothing but relax. What a great place and only an hour from home. No mice...did our three legged, slow dog, Barney, keep them away?

Next day, leaving. I hoped to have enough water left to mop but filled water jugs instead. My thoughts are: this is a great thing, even if the fees don't cover the maintenance, the experience that the Chetco Ranger District is providing for the public is so gratifying that the goodwill and publicity created should pay off in the long run. Experiences like this cannot be measured monetarily.

August 5 - Eric and Friend; St. Louis, MO and Eugene, OR

(Eric, age 13) Here's a few tips if you're going to stay here overnight. Sleep on the cabinet tops, not the floor. No mice, so don't freak out. Hang your food on the red hook in the middle of the room.

Chopping wood is fun but madrone wood is hard. Light the candles at night, it makes it really **groovy**!

August 6 - Kurt and Beth; Central Point, OR

(Beth) I am finding it difficult, as I sit here surrounded in beauty, to find the words to do justice to this experience. I wonder if God sits in a high place like this, in awe of his own creation? This breathtaking view serves as a reminder as to why I *love* Oregon. Oregon offers so much, from the rugged Craggies in the Kalmiopsis, to the forested mountains, to the glassy blue ocean. We don't have to die to go to paradise, we live in it!

When we arrived last evening, it was so foggy we couldn't see the privy. We relaxed. Kurt with the newspaper, me with the puzzle, which by the way, has at least all of the border pieces.

After steak dinner late in the evening, we were delighted to see that the fog was clearing.

To the west, we soon saw a red glow that intensified as the fog cleared. What a sunset! All at once the clouds settled around us to form a sea of cotton around our "lookout island." The three-quarter moon lit the room so that candles were not needed. We were too excited about the view to even sleep. We drifted off around midnight only to be awakened by "Timothy" in the woodbox. I think he was training for some jumping event in the Olympics. We're not sure, but we think he may have fallen into the bucket beside the woodbox and jumped and jumped and jumped until he got out. I never thought I would lay awake at 2 A.M. giggling over the commotion made by a little mouse.

To our delight, we awoke to overcast skies but no fog. It's incredible to know that the ocean is fourteen miles away and we can see small boats and the wake they are leaving. The ocean is flat and glassy. We have spent the morning going from window to window with the binoculars, taking in the scenery. Kurt has taken a panoramic photo. No one will believe this view without the proof of the photo. My only regret is that we can only stay one night.

Thank you to the USFS for providing this experience. But most of all, thank you Kurt, the man I love, for sharing your love of nature with me.

To those who follow, enjoy, enjoy, enjoy!

(Kurt) We really don't want to leave and thought about staying until the next party came in. However, remembering how nice it was arriving with no one here, we will be gone at 11:59:59. This lookout is one of the better ideas the outfit has had in years.

P.S. Beware, the mountain air does strange things to you. Beth is chopping kindling and I just finished sweeping the floor.

August 8 - Mark L.; Oakridge, OR

Chetco RD is commended for taking the gamble that this endeavor would work. The journals indicate that there's been a lot of happy campers up here and the facility is still in good shape.

There's a boulder near the trailhead at the parking area that has some great porphyritic mica.

This journal speaks the truth about wind and nocturnal critters.

August 8 and 9 - Michael, Caren, Sarah (6), Charles (3) and Hannah (1) L.; Eugene, OR

After a failed attempt to reach Snow Camp Lookout last year (see 9/3/91), we returned this year hopeful to complete the "adventure" as the children call it. At least the FS got smart and gave up relying on the US mail to get the lookout key to hopeful inhabitants. Let's hear it for combination locks.

This year we took off in sunshine from Eugene, heading for Snow Camp Mountain. The children were more excited about going to the beach but we were going to make it to the lookout, no matter what.

With our trusty forest service map of the Siskiyou National Forest, Michael behind the wheel, and me behind the map (with graduate work in geography and having taught courses at the University of Oregon in map interpretation and cartography, that seemed the logical job for me), we took off up Hunter Creek Road for attempt #2 at the assault on Snow Camp Mountain. Well, I must have given all my map reading skills to the students fifteen years ago, because I had us seven miles up the wrong road within minutes (if you can call what we were driving on a road).

Started back at the beginning of the road and with considerable lack of confidence, tried again. Luckily, the little ones were asleep so we didn't hear the cries of, "Are we there yet?" and "I want to go to the beach." It wasn't till I saw a sign that said Snow Camp Lookout that I regained that lost confidence in my map reading ability. (This must be why I became a lawyer...I can't do ordinary, mundane things that everyone else can do with ease.)

Arrived at the lookout, looked up the steep hill and thought of all the junk I'd packed. Michael loaded up the wheelbarrow...several times...and I put the one-year-old on my back and up and down we went several times with the three and six year olds in tow.

We finally made it to our goal, a year late, but well worth it.

We had planned on sleeping on the floor, but after hearing about "Timothy" the mouse, reconsidered. Unfortunately, no cots, one bed and three squirming children didn't look promising for a good night's sleep. You can push the two low cabinets together over by the west window...it's hard but close to the size of a twin bed. Most comfortable when two of the three squirming children decide that is the bed to sleep in (with Mom, of course). Who comes to the mountains for a comfortable night's sleep anyway?

Everything said about this place is true, even "Timothy" the mouse, scampering around at 3 A.M.

Put everyone to sleep last night by reading about everyone else's adventures here. A visit without children would be so peaceful and restful. You can't baby proof this 12' x 12' room! Now it's time to try and clean up this disaster of a lookout mess the kids have made. Maybe next year we'll be able to take all those great hikes everyone else has written about.

Whoever located the potty overlooking that magnificent view really had an appreciation for relief! One suggestion though, a short three foot timber retaining wall in front of the privy may save a child's life someday. We made it OK, but a constant worry.

And now it's off to the beach, so these crying kids will be happy—sure....

(Michael) What mouse? I slept like a log. Wonderful experience. We'll be back! (signed Michael, the geologist and driver.)

August 9 and 10 - Don and Shuly

The local residents (mice) were really entertaining. They seem to know their way around.

Hot in Medford today, 110 degrees.

Enjoy and leave same as you found it.

August 11 and 12 - Nancy, Kevin, Alyssa (3) and Randy (11) M.; Brookings, OR

(Randy) I agree with the person who said that the FS gives a new meaning to the word "strenuous." I'm a big Trekkie, Trekker, Trekologist, Trekaholic and all around Star Trekker.

By the way, do you know if you yell loud enough to the east of the building, you create an echo? Bye, gotta go.

P.S. Watch out for "Timothy" the mouse. I have a sister named Lissy who is three. Oh yeah, we watched the Perseids meteor shower at 10 P.M. last night and at 3 to 4 A.M.

(Nancy) We awoke this morning to the sun blazing in our eyes. It is 8:30 and eighty degrees. At 10 P.M. last night, it was eighty degrees. It didn't cool down inside until midnight. We had none of the "promised" wind but at 4 A.M. when Kevin, Randy and I were watching for the Perseids meteor showers, it had chilled down to seventy-eight degrees with a nice breeze kicking up. Of course, Lissy nursed to sleep at 10:15 P.M. or so and slept all night so she popped up at 7:30 A.M. and promptly woke Randy and I. She missed the "medium thowers" as she called them and we won't tell her that (but she and I saw the first shooting star streak across at 10 P.M.).

I was up until 4 A.M. (Kevin and Alyssa being deep sleepers, unaffected by the heat). Randy and I tossed and turned until we shed various layers of clothing (no, we didn't need all the jackets we hauled up the hill), and it cooled a little. I was high on the full moon (by which I was able to write in my journal without flashlight), and with the feeling of contentment in this place.

Since we are so close to Brookings, this feels like an extension of "home," like an extension of our backyard. This summer I have finally had time to enjoy the river and the beach, and after three years of teaching, I am taking a year off. The stress and pressure have gone from my life. We moved to Brookings three years ago, one week before school, when Alyssa was six months old. This summer has finally made Brookings begin to feel like "home." Kevin and I have a dream to both work part-time and I hope this comes true next year.

But, on to "Timothy." I forget now when I first heard him rummaging around in the woodbox, probably midnight, when I was reading Carl Sandburg's biography of Abe Lincoln. I tapped on the window and shined the flashlight a few times. At one point, he came over to the sideboard next to the bed (on the west wall). I thought I heard him munching and this morning we discovered I was right! He chewed a little of the paper towel roll (we forgot a snack for him), and maybe some of our foam bedroll (but his relatives in our garage also did that so I'm not sure if he added any distinctive touches or not). He left some calling cards there and one offering on Kevin's KURY (local radio station), hat (luckily on top)! Kevin and Randy heard him too. They also saw deer last night around the picnic table about 4 A.M.

The sunset last night was beautiful, a narrow band of crimson through the fog below and clouds above. The sunrise was more spectacular, crimson spread all over the eastern sky, speckled with clouds in rolling formations.

Lord, I give you thanks for the abundance that is mine.

I enjoyed the journal entries.

August 13, 14, 15 and 16 - Dick and Peggy B. and Mark and Carolyn W. (starting August. 14); North Bend, OR

(Dick) We made it back. The trip down the coast was real nice. It became even better in Port Orford at the rest area. Watched a gray whale calf play for fifteen to twenty minutes.

Just as beautiful as last year. It seems greener this year. Just as hot. I replaced the indoor thermometer. My daughter broke the one last year.

It is just my wife and I for a day and a half, until our good friends show up. This year, no mother-in-law and NO kids!

We drove to the pond directly below the lookout. On our way back up, we followed our friends up. The quiet and solitude was excellent while it lasted but I would much rather share it with my friends. What I would give to live up here. I would be content. What an inspiration for my knife making.

(Carolyn) We played a game of Pictionary after dark, falling asleep about 10 p.m. At 5 A.M., we heard a small mouse Dick and Peggy had seen and fed the previous day; we call him "Timothy."

About 10 A.M., we headed to Windy Valley. The hike down to Windy

Creek took about one hour and one soda pop and nuts, at the bottom.

It was beautiful and worth the hike. We then headed back up. Marc went ahead and didn't stop! Peggy and I kept stopping to catch our breath and have a drink. We filled up the empty pop can with water from the creek and poured it over our heads to keep cool on the way up.

The rest of the afternoon was lazy and we will be thinking of the steaks, salad and corn on the cob for dinner. Sure wish we had a chocolate sundae for dessert but with the view here who needs the luxuries!!!

We're all packed up and ready to go. Just one last look around is in order. We left about seven gallons of fresh water we brought up and want the next people to know it's safe to drink. We had a great time and my last words are "it's serene."

August 16 and 17 - Cecil and Doris O.; Medford, OR

After dark, the deer visited the picnic table looking for leftovers. During the night, mice in the woodbox became quite active. An occasional kick to the woodbox quiets them down for awhile.

August 17 - Jeff, Kim and Eric; Medford, OR

Climbing the last 200 feet by foot only showed us how in shape we aren't and how many fewer things to bring the next time around. Ah yes, we shall return.

When one talks about a piece of heaven on earth, they must have been speaking about here.

I've read so much about "Timothy" and his friends that I'm anxiously awaiting his/her appearance. We've already seen Chip and Dale but not the infamous "Timothy."

The sun is gone now, making room for a kaleidoscope of stars that fill the clear heavens. We're so used to living in the city, even a city the size of Medford, we are awed by the number of stars that are visible. The end of a precious day has brought a splendidly spectacular night.

(10 P.M.) We notice an orange glow in the east. Knowing how dry it is, we first think it is a forest fire, but in less than a minute we realize what it is…it's the three-quarter moon peeking over the horizon. Soon it is hovering above the landscape, a big orange ball with its craters clearly visible through binoculars.

Spending time here clearly indicated how beautiful this planet is and how important it is to protect. I hope you will note that you can see some places that have been clear cut. It's truly sad to see.

We didn't use all of our water so we left it as well. The .22 shell casings we found (most by Eric), made excellent poker chips.

We saw a peregrine falcon. Last year we were up this way and the FS helped take us in to do a news story about the falcon. At the time it was endangered and only seven were known to exist. I'm sure they are still endangered, but I do believe that more are accounted for.

I don't think "Timothy" is too keen on BBQ potato chips!

August 21 - Brian and George; Porterville, CA

"TIMOTHY" DOESN'T LIVE HERE ANYMORE.

"Timothy" was a bothersome pest,
We looked and looked till we found his nest,
It wasn't long till he was laid to rest,
"Timothy" will never, never bother another guest!

(Author's note: the following comments on the same page were made later by at least four other guests.)

"Timothy" had more right to be here than **you!** JERKS!

Since when is it OK for the guest to murder the host?

Only the two-legged have become **pests** to all life. Where is the harmony?

Hang your food!

Probably the same damned Californian who cut down all the trees! Thanks for the great view of all the clear cuts.

As if Oregon hasn't cut any???? Flown to Portland lately?

(Author's note: The alleged death of "Timothy" seems to have stirred up the guests and his departure took some harmony with it.)

August 22 - Diane, Joan and Clav; Eugene and Marcola, OR

We are happy to say that the ghost of "Timothy" is alive and well and that his sister, "Alice" has taken up where he left off. She politely ate what we left out for her and went on her merry way to let us sleep in peace.

The sun peeked through the fog by 9 A.M. and we were greeted by the song of a quail nearby. Gorgeous warm day. We hiked to Windy Valley and saw a bandtailed pigeon and a wrentit.

"Alice" is also training for the Olympics, jumping up and down to get to higher places after carting off the treats we left her by the woodpile. She stayed away from the sleeping people on the floor and had a real good time in the woodbox. She was fun to watch with the flashlight and added pleasure to this marvelous weekend!

58

What a wonderful way to get away from it all! Loved reading the historical stuff and learning how to spot fires on the firefinder.

P.S. We now know where the phrase "don't spit into the wind" comes from—brushing our teeth.

August 24 and 25 - Tom and Betty B.; Eugene, OR

When I tried to envision what we would do for forty-eight hours in a lookout, I never considered writing in a lookout journal. But I've already spent the first half day reading the entries of others…so I guess I'll add to the verbiage. (How do they have time to hike when it takes so long to read this journal?)

Betty and I are here to celebrate our nineteenth anniversary. What a perfect way to do it. As much as we love our four daughters, we are really appreciating being away from them. We have time to focus on our own relationship for a change. This is a great time too, for resting up before the onslaught of activities that accompany the beginning of the school year. We've even had time to talk a little about our goals and priorities for the coming year, between reading journal entries, of course!

Regarding "Timothy": We're pretty sure the August 21st entry was a fictional attempt to incite the anger of the world's mouse lovers and it appears to have succeeded! In the few hours we've been here since the sun went down, "Timothy" has appeared as predicted by many other journal entries. Tonight, so far, he appears to prefer the open windowsill to the woodbox.

I work in the forests of the east part of Lane County, so breathtaking vistas aren't a rare sight to me. They still bring great joy, however, and experiencing this beauty and solitude with my wife, in a vacation mode, is especially nice. The stars are striking, too, though it's too cold in the wind to stay out and look for long. The whole thing is a very satisfying experience.

O Lord…How majestic is Your name in all the earth! You have set your glory above the heavens. From the lips of children and infants (and "Timothy" the mouse), you have ordained praise. When I consider your heavens, the work of your fingers, the moon and the stars, which you set in place, what is man that you are mindful of him?…that you care for him? Psalm 8 (parts).

After reading about everyone else's active life-styles when they're up here on the mountain, I guess I have to admit to a little laziness. We don't plan to do any hiking or driving or climbing or **anything**. I wasn't even going to walk down to my van today, except a USFS guy came up to tell me I had a flat tire. (My spare had air – Yay!) That van (a VW Vanwagon), has twelve years and 160,000 miles on it and I don't think it's ever had a flat before. Oh yeah, my Coleman stove quit working, too (after nineteen years), so I had to go to the van anyway to get some oil (I only had motor oil), to try to get the pump working. And it worked (for a while anyway; I'm not so good at fixing things long term).

Other than that little bit of excitement, and picking up glass fragments from the parking area, and some old garbage around the lookout, and splitting a little wood, we have done nothing! It's good, for me anyway, to get in touch with my wife and talk about life and beauty and silence and kids and humidity and pressure gradients and mice, etc. And she has a great attitude too, when the tire's flat and the stove is broke.

Life. I see it in terms of relationships; relationship with God, with your family and with others in the world around you. Sitting up here in the lookout, I'm tempted to say that your relationship with nature is also important, but I think that would be a little redundant because your relationship with nature is tied in with your relationship with God. Those of us whose idea of God is based on Judeo-Christian teaching tend to think of the beauty around us as manifestations of God's power, love, beauty and creativity. Those who reject the Judeo-Christian concept of God (and this is admittedly conjecture on my part, since it is not my particular belief system), often tend to view nature as "Nature" or God or a deity unto itself. I think nature is resilient and powerful. I don't see it as mystical or fragile. I think some people love nature so much that they don't see it clearly. They mistake beauty for fragility, as men sometimes do with women.

Looking at the trees up here, on the east side of this ridge, it appears that wind from the east is the dominant force during the growing season, based on how the branches grow.

Below the lookout on the east is a dead tree that seems to be embracing a live tree. Or is the live tree holding up the dead tree? It seems to symbolize how life and death are interrelated.

August 29 and 30 - Paul L. and Jo B.; Sutherlin, OR

What a magnificent panorama. A person could travel all around the world and not find any scenery so spectacular.

By 7:30 P.M. the wind had come up in wild gusts and I was getting very apprehensive. We blew out the candles and I thought the roof might blow off at any minute with the noise it made. Sleep overcame me and before long the sun was peeking over the hill. It is hard to hide from its brightness and I finally got up. Paul already had the fire going and water for coffee. Bacon and eggs tasted so good.

Yes, "Timothy" or "Alice" were out and about. One of them jumped on the bed next to Paul and whipped his tail around by his neck. Perhaps the mouse was just thanking us for the bread we put out.

We enjoyed the time to just be lazy, write letters, video tape the scenery, read and write in the journals. Great experience!

August 31 and September 1 - Tom D.; Medford, OR

Arrived about 2:30 from Medford with two adults in the front of a small Mazda pickup with a hyperactive cocker spaniel and three kids in a camper shell (almost as hyperactive), via the Smith River Highway. Beautiful weather with a little wind and a billion stars. The kids had a visit last night from "Timothy," or "Alice" or whoever. Awoke this morning to fog and drizzle. Glad we had the view yesterday.

September 1, 2 and 3 - John; Medford, OR

Unlike those who have honeymooned here, celebrated anniversaries, announced a new baby or watched a child's first steps, I am here by myself. Have been here since 1 P.M. and have experienced a gradual relaxation that is very beautiful. I live a very stressful, hectic life and this place is a dream come true.

This is a great place to visit totally alone. Although I can think of several people with whom I would like to share this experience, I am amazed at how much I am enjoying my own company.

(4:15) Driving to the other end of Windy Valley trail turned out to be a good idea. Good trail; saw grouse, blue tailed skink, snakes, bear signs, coyote signs and elk and deer signs. Swam in ice cold water. Had to leave in a hurry due to thunderstorm. It is heading this way. There is absolutely no breeze. Almost constant thunder coming from Red Mountain area.

Fantastic storm! Put on a show for over an hour before hitting here. Lots of thunder and lightning and hard wind from the east. Several strikes in the canyon below. The storm passed, the wind stopped for thirty minutes. Then came a hard, cold wind from the west. Low clouds and fog rolled in, the temperature dropped and the wind stopped again.

I really hate to leave this place. I plan to tell absolutely no one about this place. It will only be a matter of time until there's a five-year waiting list.

September 4 - James, Gwen, Jon and Miah; Corvallis, OR

At 7:20 last night we spotted smoke to the west, two valleys over, just this side of the Big Craggies. About 8:30 P.M. a Forest Service person showed up. After pinpointing the location of the fire with compass and maps, "they" decided to let it wait until morning. We can still see smoke this morning.

September 5 and 6 - Greg and Cindy E.; Bandon, OR

We spotted the fire on the east side of the South Fork of Collier Creek. It started by lightning on September 4, from the same lightning storm that started the Horse Fire just south of Horse Sign Butte. The smoldering fire out in Collier Creek now seems to be sitting at the SE corner of section 23. The firefinder lines up at an azimuth of 83 degrees from this lookout. It looks like it's right on the edge of the Big Craggies botanical area, well within the wilderness (T 37 S., R 12 W., Sec 23, SE ¼ of SE ¼ of SE ¼).

The serenity and pause afforded by our time here is something I look forward to again. May the rest of the world find the space and time to reflect as we have while here at Snow Camp.

Double bed is nice improvement!

September 6 and 7 - Bradley and Diane; Grants Pass, OR

(Bradley) Only a few sightings: one Sasquatch (Bigfoot), two ferocious "Timothys," airplanes, trucks and boats on the ocean. I hate to go back to work tomorrow. I'm definitely coming back next year before the big wedding day. Notice, I mentioned the Sasquatch; last night around 3:30 A.M. one came asking for a cup of sugar and said if I didn't come up with it, he'd go tell his buddy the "Ax Murderer" and "Timothy the Terrible Tyrant" to pay us a visit, but we were lucky...we gave him a bite of our submarine sandwiches and he went on his merry way.

September 7, 8, 9, 10 and 11 - Scott and Erin; Scholls, OR

It was quiet until the dogs started barking an "alert." Ten minutes later a hunter with a bow shows up, dressed in full camo with face paint and "scented" too, no doubt. It would have been more intimidating if his wife/girlfriend wasn't accompanying him. He "scoped" out the area with his binoculars. We let the dogs bark constantly to let them know we didn't appreciate their presence. With each dog weighing in at over 100 pounds apiece, our fortress in the clouds looks well protected.

(September 8) Awoke this morning at 5 A.M. to the sounds of the wind wrapping its arms around Snow Camp Mountain. Orion looked down from his place in the southern sky, his bejeweled belt glistening in a galaxy of blue-black velvet. The sun is promising its arrival to the east, grabbing bits of the Milky Way and taking back the night. Still sleepy, I blink to close my eyes and...in that moment, Orion shot a razor-thin streak of orange. A shooting star in retaliation to morning's mantle. This place is surreal!

(September 9) The wind blew all night! The lookout shook and the guy wires rattled, **_all night!!_** I kept murmuring in my sleep, "please stop." It was frightening for me. But as I looked up to check on the dogs, they were fast asleep, as was Scott. I guess I'm a light sleeper (i.e., wimp). The wind blew hard until noon, then it simply died...it's hot without the wind.

Back to society and mankind tomorrow. We'll lay over in Salishan near Lincoln City. Then home to the farm...it'll be nice. We've been camping since August 31. It's been a good time to ask ourselves if we're doing what we enjoy, living our lives the way we want to. Lots of times we wished we could be a lookout...(circa 1940s), being a ranger, being a vintner, being anything but high tech workaholics.

This was a good time for the peace of our souls!

September 11 and 12 - Melynda and Michael P.; Silverton, OR

Have had this "getaway" planned for so long I was afraid the anticipation would dwarf the actual experience, but it's everything I've dreamed of. Now that the two Forest Service guys are gone, we'll have the complete silence to enjoy the bliss of each other's company, something that's been hard to come by since MANY years ago.

(7:40 P.M.) Oooh, we are so lucky to enjoy the full moon rising in the east as the sun simultaneously sets over the Pacific. The last time we were somewhere to enjoy that sight together was sixteen years ago, September 1976, when we met! The wind is rising but the wood stove keeps it cozy in here...thank goodness.

(3 A.M.) Now we know why so many people are up at this time writing in the journal. We're not in Kansas any more, Toto! Woke up to the bed rockin'...and it wasn't us! I laid awake chanting "It's been here since 1958. It's part of the experience." Then we gave it up and got up, stoked the fire and made some Swiss Mocha. The stars and moon are beautiful but it's doing some serious blowing. Even "Timothy" won't surface tonight! We can see the lights of Crescent City and lights twinkling out on the ocean. Dawn is just hours away. We'll see if the wind lets up. Good luck, tomorrow night's guests. It *is* an experience!

September 13, 14 and 15 - Lile and Richard; Rogue River, OR

I sat outside late last night, wrapped in a blanket, on the picnic table and let the moonlight cleanse my soul. I am so thankful for moments like these.

Enjoy! This is a very special place.

September 17, 18 and 19 - Len K.; Dearborn, MI

TOUR GUIDE: We arrived here as all who have come before us, from the bottom to the top. Arrivals from the top have been undetected or at least unreported. I made it a point to look around so I took a chair out to the catwalk and looked awhile at Big Craggies. It was then that I noticed my tour guide. I wasn't expecting a tour guide, let alone one that wanted to lead the tour from the tip of my right toe. I decided "ocean view" might not have guided tours, so I went there, taking my chair. Slow day at the Snow Camp— the same tour guide showed up as if to say, "So you've found the ocean more to your liking." I tried the Mt. Emily view with the same results, walked around the catwalk twice in each direction, walked inside, grabbed a flyswatter and went back to the Big Craggies. Placing the flyswatter across my lap, tapping it on the arm rest or my chair when another tour was about to be offered. The guide must have noticed my unconcealed weapon because there were no noticeable tours the rest of the day. The sun set, the moon rose. I know what these things are. I went to public school.

(September 18) PANCAKE SUNSET: My friend and traveling companion told me that people can live on eggs and bananas. I thought this to be novel so I did indeed bring eggs and bananas. Today I remembered that I still had pancake syrup left from the initial purchase of groceries in Portland. The beauty of it was, I had already rationed and accepted my decision on how to make eggs and bananas last for three days. Now I have the option of having pancakes for no reason at all. Tonight the sun set like one giant pancake and darkness fell upon it like a heavy maple syrup.

September 20 - Maya, Snow and Myray; Williams, OR

We arrived in the gusty darkness of a brilliant starlit sky. It is the dark side of the moon so the stars are brilliant. We held tight to our three month baby, Myray, and climbed the hill with our bare essentials. It is warm. The wind has Myray very awake. We lit candles, burnt some sage and began to relax. It is Snow's thirty-fifth birthday.

We have many fond memories of being here on June 11 and 12, just before Myray was born, but we spent that time in the white fog, rain and wind. (It did clear up for fifteen minutes just before sunset.)

We lie in bed watching for meteors. POW, WOW, ZOWIE.

I too am saddened by the killing of "Timothy." Such annoyance and such power. But I know that these killers will find their lesson around the next corner so I keep my mind and heart free from anger.

We are still in this moment, baby just went to sleep, dad is reading a newspaper, sipping organic coffee. I'm having some fruit juice and some of this very, very fresh air. I give thanks for this special spot on top of the world. I am Maya.

September 24 - Graig and Barbara D.; Cave Junction, OR

(7:15 P.M.) The sun has just set over the Pacific, and it's blowing like hell. Can't say they didn't warn us. By the shape of the trees and shrubs around the lookout, it doesn't take a rocket scientist to figure out the weather is harsh.

Ah, but what a room with a view!

This is a one night adventure for us while we're on a seed collecting venture. We have a nursery in the Illinois Valley, somewhere due east of here, just beyond the Kalmiopsis Wilderness. We grow native trees and shrubs for replanting in fire accesses and places where the U.S. Forest Service wants to replant food species for wildlife habitat.

Unlike earlier visitors, we have not had the heat, flies, or fleas. Nor have we seen "Timothy" the mouse. We did see a bobcat on our drive here. This is the second one that we've seen on our seed collecting trips. Wow! What a neat creature. Also, deer and elk hunting season must be close at hand as we have not seen any. Others have left great entries and it's doubtful that we can compete. But we will leave something a bit different for those interested in discovering what those shrubbery plants are around the lookout.

[Inserted were various samples]

1. Golden Chinquapin (*Castanopsis crysophylla*) Nuts are good to eat if you can get them out of the spiny husk without hurting yourself.
2. Hairy Manzanita *(Arctostaphylos columbiana)*
   Note—there are other species of manzanita here too.
3. Huckleberry Oak (*Quercus vaccinifolia*)
4. Sadler Oak (*Quercus sadleriana*)

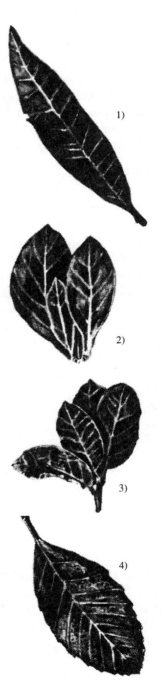

1)

2)

3)

4)

(September 25) Our stay at the lookout has been as wonderful as that mentioned by everyone else. We did get a surprise visit last night about 8:30 P.M. from a state trooper. (Uh…officer, aren't you a bit off your regular beat?) As it turned out, he wanted to use the lookout to spot illegal deer hunters who use spotlights. As we had rented this place, we suggested, politely, that he choose another vantage point. The trees include Douglas fir and at least two types of pines. Can't get close enough to identify the pine species.

Remember, there's more to a forest than trees. It's an ecosystem where all plants hold a purpose.

September 31 - Scott and Lisa; Lake Oswego, OR

Like others before us we're having a viewless experience up here. **No** regrets!

There's been a raging wind and driving rain since we arrived, making this little box about the coziest little haven we could imagine. The Coleman lantern lit the cloud fog in window shapes, all around us…strange, like stationary, almost touchable northern lights. I think what makes this whiteout so pleasant for me is that as it brightens (thins from the top, but never reveals sun or sky), it gives the peripheral impression of a snow scene drenched in sunshine, like Maine in winter dress. Last winter in Lake Oswego, we had two frosts that melted by noon and I miss the snows of Casco Bay. Still, Oregon has claimed us forever.

Now, housekeeping. When we arrived we found the mattress soaked from the leaking windows. We've pulled the bed away and have attempted to dry the mattress by the stove. Tricky to do. We're leaving the bed away from the windows in case it rains again.

Spent time designing mini cabin for us in later years, so inspired!

October 1, 2 and 3 - Richards; Medford, OR

End of Season.

Arrived here in clouds and mist, no wind. First night, clouds all around the horizon, none directly overhead. Second night, clouds directly overhead and none on the horizon, no wind. Third night, 100 mph winds, no clouds. We flew a kite, sort of. It was like a Three Stooges comedy routine and ended up on the roof. It cost ninety-eight cents including string.

Second day I heard voices and wondered if I was becoming schizo-phrenic. A man and a woman were on the knoll to the north of the cabin, videotaping us, etc. I was not dressed. I got dressed in a fury and they actually walked right up here smiling and saying they just thought they'd come up and say hello, if that was OK. I said it was not OK. They shrugged, muttering something about hospitality and walked back on down the road.

Isn't that astonishing? I wonder of those who read these words, how many will be offended at my behavior and how many will be offended at their behavior? I find it incredible that anyone would think I came all this way and locked a gate behind me just so that two complete strangers could drop by and have a chat? Do some of you really think I was crude and rude? I was exhibiting considerable restraint. My wife was disappointed I didn't greet them in the nude. I wish I'd thought of it.

There are hummingbirds up here, though not in this wind here at the moment. This weather is much preferable to high summer with its bugs and heat even if the wind does make it sound like trolls are bowling on the roof.

Interesting that we should encounter a camcorder junkie and no hunters. Did you ever notice how often these morons film totally motionless subjects? This clown actually filmed the brass geological marker set in the stone! I can imagine how interested his friends will be in seeing that on several feet of motion picture film. Grateful grandchildren too, no doubt.

Otherwise, this has proved to be the personal and internal experience it should be. No more crowded campgrounds. Isn't my tolerance level awful? Of course, contrasts are what make life yummy!

This evening we will go see *The Last of the Mohicans* in the Medford Mall Cinema and cruise the strollways and stare and giggle. I've got this amazing idea for our nineteenth wedding anniversary celebration/present. I've decided to take my wife to the 98 cent store (where I got the kite) and let her pick out anything she wants!

So, I sacrificed football for this. Of course I set the VCR for the Miami/Florida State game but the radio said there was a power outage. Anyway, I won't miss Monday night, Dallas and Philadelphia, though I do like college football better. We will be back next year, of course. I wish the season extended further into the fall so we could experience Snow Camp with snow.

Hello to all you others who've been here and contributed. Will we really have to hang out a "No Visitors" sign, or is it just me?

Let's keep this a clique and not tell anyone else about it...OK? Isn't true privacy wonderful?

That was the last entry for Snow Camp's 1992 season.

"This looks like first class seating"

TIMOTHY'S JOURNAL

May 25, 1992

Dear journal. It seems like quite some time has passed since I've made an entry. I have been so busy with last minute preparations to leave the Ranger Station and getting the "kids" settled into a routine, since we won't be around to help them out. They're old enough to be on their own, but still a little unsure of their capabilities. Sandra is acting like a typical mother, having a hard time letting go; however, we are both really looking forward to this "vacation" at Snow Camp Lookout. She is also pregnant again so we are quite anxious to get settled in. When Uncle Joe returned from Snow Camp last year, he convinced us to try it this season. It's all arranged. We'll sneak a ride on the Forest Service truck due to leave tomorrow. I found a way into the Snow Camp cooking utensil box in the storeroom.

I overheard them say that all that stuff is to go up there and we have packed everything we want to take with us for the summer. We are having a little get together this evening with family and friends over a peanut butter and jelly sandwich (on whole wheat), which was left in the office today by one of the workers. That was nice of him to leave something so fresh and one of my favorite things, too. Isn't life grand....

June 3, 1992

Well here we are at Snow Camp and pretty well settled in. I sure am glad to get here. With the farewell gifts for us and the babies, we had to pack another suitcase. That ride up from Brookings nearly made me carsick. The road is as crooked as a dog's hind leg.

We haven't seen anyone for a few days so we are enjoying the peace and quiet. Don't know when all the renters are due but I hope they show up pretty soon as I'm looking forward to the easy food supply. Resourceful I am, but frankly I've gotten a little lazy with living around the Ranger Station in Brookings. Today I did some foraging around the lookout but it is early in the season and the pickings are slim. The nights are still quite nippy. Warm weather is slower coming at 4,223 feet.

Sandra is going to "hatch" anytime now. She is experienced at child birthing but I know she is apprehensive as we don't know anyone around here. I think she would feel better if she had a girlfriend or better yet, a mouse midwife available. She will do just fine. It's not like we haven't done this before.

We've built a very comfortable nest in the bottom of the woodbox with some toilet paper. That stuff is great! Light weight, easy to carry and it fluffs up so nicely. The Forest Service man who brought us here also chopped wood and filled the woodbox. As long as no one empties the box, we should be safe.

June 8, 1992

I'm a proud papa! Sandra gave birth to four babies, two boys and two girls. I guess they are kinda cute. I say that because they're ours and I love them, but frankly when I see other mouse babies, they strike me as...well, I don't know, a little funny looking. They are so pink and wrinkled, no hair and their eyes aren't open so they have that squinty look. But it doesn't take long for them to grow their hair and then they'll be running all over the place. (And I can't get into the way human babies look either.)

Sandra has her hands full with nursing the babies so I have my work cut out for me. My "honey do" list seems to be getting longer and longer.... Later.

June 12, 1992

The lady that left today looked very pregnant to me. They left a loaf of bread on the counter overnight so I stocked up. The plastic bag is no barrier to me though it is a little frustrating, seeing all that delicious bread and I can't haul but a little bit in one evening. If I could only get a whole loaf stashed away, I could retire for the summer! Oh, for a mouse wheelbarrow big enough to haul a half slice at a time....

June 20, 1992

I am lucky to be making this entry! My children were nearly orphans! I definitely used up one of my mouse lives a few days ago. I was out looking for crumbs or whatever I could find in broad daylight when the new renters showed up. I figured I had plenty of time as it usually takes the new people a little while before they come inside because they get hung up on the view outside. But these folks immediately opened the door upon their arrival (apparently the last people didn't lock it), and dropped their CAT on the floor! He was on me before I could move! He didn't bite me hard but I thought I'd die of a heart attack anyway. I just knew it was the end! I saw my life flash in front of my eyes. My mind raced away as I tried to think of a way out of this predicament. Should I play dead? If he'd let me up, I could do a song and dance routine, throw in a little comedy, try to reduce the tension (mine, not his). It would be a bad time to get my usual case of stage fright. I do fine just clowning around in a group but put me on a stage and "wham!" I die. Whoops, poor choice of words. What about a calling card on his tongue? Nope, don't think I can do that, I need to be relaxed...preferably with something to read.

Suddenly he just opened his mouth and I fell to the floor, landing on my feet. I took off toward the table leg but he knocked me flat with a heavy paw. It took my breath away! Pinned down, I looked right into his eyes and could detect a mischievous gleam there. I knew then that I had a chance, albeit a slim one, as he wanted to "play" with me!

From my position on the hard floor, I could see the end of his tail flicking back and forth. Funny how things can slow down in a time of crisis. That's what happened then. I could see everything so clearly, right down to the finest threads of the dust ball by my head. The stiff cat whiskers reminded me of swords I'd once seen in a book. In the

background, from the boards of the woodbox, I heard Sandra scream my name. I felt the pressure on my chest lessen and got set to make another run for it when all at once the cat was flying straight up with a surprised look on his face. I was off and running in a heartbeat and secured my escape by slipping behind the low counter. I didn't know what happened. I heard a lady scolding the "bad kitty." Sandra told me later that the lady saved my life by grabbing her cat by the scruff of its neck and lifting it into the air.

I waited for some time behind the counter until the cat went outside, then I slipped to the woodbox where we all laid low until they left the next day. The kids got their first lesson in being quiet and they did real well. I'm nursing some sore ribs, but otherwise not much worse for the wear. I'll be a lot more careful from here on out. God, how I hate cats. It's times like this I wish I was a dog...a BIG dog.

Once I had a close call with a hawk but a bird called out an alarm and I made it under a bush at the last minute. Those of us that are potential meals on wheels, look out for one another. If you figure in coyotes, bobcats, snakes, traps with cheese (and I love cheese), sticky traps and big feet, this mouse life is hazardous and sometimes short lived. I would just like to make it to old age with a house on the beach somewhere.

FOURTH OF JULY

"Ooh...Aah...Awesome..."

July 5, 1992

As any parent knows, raising kids is a lot of work! Seems like we are so busy that Sandra and I don't have much time for each other right now. It's all I can do to pilfer enough food to keep those hungry tummies full.

Had a special treat last night, chocolate. I just love chocolate! It was the first taste for the children and of course, they liked it too. Probably should have told them it was good for them, like vegetables, then they wouldn't have tried it.

There was an exciting and beautiful light show towards Brookings last night. Started right after dark, which is when my work really begins. While the humans sat on the deck to watch, we sat on the inside windowsill. The kids had a great time, as you could tell from the "Oohs" and "Aahs." They kept saying "Awesome!" Now where did they get that?

July 9, 1992

This woodbox is a good place to live, although there are a few drawbacks. Recently a human started a number of fires in the stove in order to cook their food. I suspect they were having problems with their portable cook stove. It made this place very warm and I was experiencing a little panic, and I feared they would discover our nest in the bottom of the woodbox. Fortunately, they filled the woodbox before it was empty, but every armful of wood dropped in the box was like an earthquake!

Sandra has been able to get away from the nest more lately because the kids are getting old enough to be left alone for awhile. She discovered some fragrant sticks that she really likes. I don't know what they are but I saw a human lighting the end of one in the outhouse.

She asked me to bring her some but I couldn't pack a whole one...I had to chew a portion off. Yuck! It tastes awful. Smells good though. With that scent on her fur, it tends to make us romantic. Next thing you know, we'll have some more children!

July 16, 1992

A funny looking box created quite a stir with the children. It was black with push buttons, had a shiny rod that extended upwards from the back and plastic cartridges that the young humans put into it. It made a lot of noise and when my kids heard the racket they started tapping their feet and dancing around. The kids were glued to the crack in the woodbox where they could see it when they weren't kicking up dust. I found it hard to get them to do their chores when that thing was making noise.

July 22, 1992

Smelled chocolate in some cookies. Just about drove me crazy...crazy enough to venture out in broad daylight!

I'm amazed at the power little ol' me has over some big ol' humans, particularly the female ones. I think some are afraid of me because they get all flighty, sometimes emitting a piercing scream; and they get up on the furniture with their feet off the floor. Sometimes it goes to my head and I boldly run around the place like I own it. Sandra says, "Quit showing off."

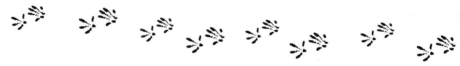

August 6, 1992

Another crisis at Snow Camp. Eric, my most adventuresome son, fell into the plastic mop bucket last night. He was jumping up and down hollering, "Dad! Dad!" I kept telling him to settle down and be quiet before he attracted the attention of the humans, but he was frightened and wouldn't listen to me. It took quite awhile for me to figure out how to get him out, but finally I hit upon the idea of a rope of some sort. I do hope the man isn't too upset about part of his shoelace missing.

August 12, 1992

There was a bill cap that I truly coveted. Too large for me, but I do wish I had one my size. I left the man my calling card to let him know how much I liked his hat.

Built a new nest in the other corner of the woodbox with some more of that soft tissue. We abandon our old nests. We never clean our houses...we just move.

August 17, 1992

Boy, am I tired. Didn't get much rest last night as the man kept kicking the woodbox.

August 19, 1992

For the first time, I found a food I don't like — BB-Q potato chips! How can anyone eat those things? Give me chocolate any day....

August 22, 1992

We went for a picnic and combined it with a foraging lesson for the kids. When we returned, our nest was gone. The people had obviously removed all the wood in order to get to our home. I shudder to think what would have happened if we had been in the box. I'll rebuild as soon as possible. Thank goodness it's summer and not too cold at night.

The man seemed like a mean one. Very few humans are like that. I find that most are really OK. Up here at Snow Camp, the average person is pretty nice.

August 24, 1992

I've nearly got the new nest done, made out of pieces of paper towels. Not as nice as toilet paper but we are not complaining. Got the boys to help me on this project... that's why it's going so fast.

76

August 30, 1992

Again I'll say it…the people that visit Snow Camp are overall a really nice bunch. This last couple left us some bread. It wasn't an accident, they purposely set it out for us. I went to their bed and said "Thank you" as best I knew how.

September 7, 1992

I got an unexpected ride to Brookings. A Forest Service employee came up to check things out, and I decided to check out what was in his vehicle. I was smelling his lunch sack when he shut the door and drove off. Thank goodness he went to a place I knew and could get a ride back to Sandra and the kids. While I was there, I caught up on the news and was pumped thoroughly by aunt Myrtle. She can be ruthless. Another good reason to get back to Snow Camp. Caught a ride back three days later. Sandra was worried sick. Had quite the reunion…so happy to see each other. I'll bet there are more children coming now….

**TIMOTHY IN
THE LUNCH SACK**

**"I'm going to be late for
dinner now!"**

"Hi, Lady"

September 27, 1992

Summer is winding down. The nights are getting colder, which is more noticeable at this elevation. We'll be sad to leave but sure don't want to spend the winter here. Food could be as scarce as hen's teeth.

Had some more fun last night. A couple was sleeping in the bed with the lady lying next to the window, her face very close to the glass. I'd heard her say earlier that she was disappointed about not seeing me. Knowing how much she wanted to meet me, I thought I'd let her get a good look. I ran around on the outside window ledge, got right in front of her face and then threw my body up against the glass with a thud. She awoke with a start and saw me spread-eagled just inches from her nose. I'm afraid I frightened her, but when she got over her initial start, I hope she realized it was just a joke. I laughed so hard I nearly fell off the ledge. She woke the man when she bolted upright, so I didn't stick around long. Sandra scolded me for my actions before she broke down and laughed with me! Mouse humor....

October 4, 1992

Well, the Forest Service people are here and you can tell they are closing Snow Camp for the winter. They are busy washing windows, packing boxes, cleaning house and preparing to put the shutters on the outside. I suspect they'll be leaving tomorrow and we must go with them. I've got a way into a box that they have already packed so we'll all ride down in that.

This has been the best place in the world for a mouse and his family to spend the summer. Great views, good food, good company, warm and dry. A mouse couldn't ask for more.

Well, just one more thing and I believe my wish has just been granted. I smell chocolate!!!

TIMOTHY and SANDRA —
We'll be back!

SNOW CAMP JOURNAL — 1993

June 14 and 15 - Nick, Patricia and John (11) F.; Tidewater, OR

A new season. We arrived at 12:45 P.M. Fog moving in. We were sure it would lift. Wrong! Thank you for the wheelbarrow. Nick only had to make four trips. I followed behind just in case he lost anything and John was far ahead, afraid he might have to help. We were here two years ago and enjoyed it and said we would be back. Here we are. We were hoping to come last year but Nick being a USFS firefighter, was gone all summer but one day (in four months). We said, "No matter what," this year we would get our vacation in.

(4 P.M.) Very muggy (eighty degrees), no wind, fog completely around us. We read the journals from the time we were here two years ago. Great reading.

(June 15, 11 A.M.) Well, the fog has lifted enough to see the outhouse and table. We're going hiking anyway. Hope we'll be able to find our way back before tomorrow.

We made it down to Snow Camp Meadow. Half way down it cleared for us. We realized we were in the clouds. The hike was cool. We saw elk tracks that were real fresh. We walked to the north end of the meadow and saw four elk (three cows and a bull). Then, as they saw us there, more came out front. We counted seventeen of those beautiful creatures (four bulls and the rest cows). We watched for about five minutes before they disappeared. We tried to track them but no luck.

Chip and Dale came this afternoon and finished off John's pancakes we left on the picnic table. "Timothy" or "Alice" hasn't shown up and I really hope they'll wait for the next renters.

June 18, 19, 20 and 21 - Joan and Larry; Eugene, OR

We are spending Larry's fiftieth birthday at Snow Camp, our first of two weekends planned here this summer.

The 360 degree vista is awesome! Our new telescope helps us see in the distance, not to mention the stars. There are so many more stars than the naked eye can see!

We hiked down to Snow Camp Meadow, had lunch and spent the afternoon wandering among the tall grass and wildflowers.

Our only visitors have been hummingbirds, tree swallows, bees, mosquitoes and centipedes...counted eighty coming up "the hill."

Glad we experienced some of the different conditions and recognize it's easy for us to say when nearly all of our stay was sunny and beautiful. It helps, though, to come prepared for either way and accept the beauty of however it is. Be back in August.

Suggestions: (1) Don't feed the animals, it just encourages them to come looking for food and human food is not good for them. (2) Keep food put away (top shelves preferably) so rodents cannot easily get into. If they get into yours, they'll return looking for others. (3) Screens would be nice.

The wheelbarrow is a life saver.

June 23 - Peter and Teresa; Kelso, WA

Fire spotted before arrival to Snow Camp. Fire is fifteen acres, probably slash burn after all.

We just came back from Snow Camp and Fairview meadows. We couldn't find a foot trail to Snow Camp Meadow. After we returned from the meadows, we found good directions in the July 3, 4, 5 and 6, 1991 entries in the journal. Should of read the journal first.

June 24 and 25 - Suzy and Dave; Portland, OR

We arrived to the sight of centipedes, in how shall I say, compromising positions (conjugal activity). The wind started to blow and the cabin was like a ship without an anchor (and the sea around, it was on fire). Sunset was God's blink and we sat and exchanged words, none of them even came close (to describing that is, etc., etc.).

Saw a bear on the way up, our metal machine scared him and he hightailed it into the woods. By the time we drove by where he was, there was only the sound of branches breaking.

Went to Fairview Meadow (rocks with various patinas and lizards). Was chased by a bee who obviously had a personal vendetta, a score to settle with me.

Cabin is beautiful. FS people must be written to and thanked for their generosity and hospitality. Thanks for sharing the mountain with us!!

Thanks to Dave for transporting me from the city to a truly awesome place full of peace and tranquillity.

June 25, 26 and 27 - Dick and Peggy V. and Marc and Carolyn W.; North Bend, OR

(Marc and Carolyn) Drank, drank, drank, and drank some more. Lemon drops — Vodka with lemon wedges rolled in sugar — Yum-Yum! Got pretty twisted and passed out, oh boy!! I'm glad we got the drinking out of the way. I don't think any of us are as young as we thought we were. Saturday morning was a struggle but we got up at seven and hiked to Snow Camp Meadow. Stream at the meadow was clear and cold; good place to cool off and relax. The hike back was a little tough.

Great radio reception!!!

(Dick and Peggy) Well, it is our third year here. I wish I could live here. This is one of the prettiest places in the northwest. We all loved the hike down to Snow Camp Meadow. Found some outrageous quartz crystals, lots of colors. We found six varieties of orchids. If you find them, leave them for others to enjoy.

What happened to the puzzles we left for others to enjoy?

No better place to be with your friends and no kids. See you next year.

June 28 and 29 - Claudia C. and Jim A.; Bend and Burns, OR

After renting Acker Rock Lookout last year we knew we were hooked! Snow Camp is wonderful too. Enjoyed watching the ocean in different moods.

The constant wind is a challenge. In three days, it howled and shook the lookout for all but three hours.

We will be at Acker Rock again next month and plan to rent others. Each is unique in its design, amenities and scenery. Check with the various National Forests because more lookouts are available to rent in Washington and Oregon.

Thank you to all who have worked and volunteered to make and keep these lookouts public.

July 3 and 4 - Bobby Y., Judi M., John and Linda G.; Grants Pass, OR

We saw the fireworks south of tower, from either Brookings or Crescent City, can't tell which. Great display from here!

The wind velocity estimates of 100 mph are very conservative. A special thanks to whoever anchored the outhouse. With these winds, tobogganing through the trees wasn't something we looked forward to.

Very little wildlife; two chipmunks, lizards, two hawks, waterdogs, two deer, and three elephants as the supply of beer and Kahlua ran low.

July 6 and 7 - Dale and Pat T.; Arcata, CA

We enjoyed a wonderful hike to Windy Valley. We drove down the main road toward Brookings, about 5.7 miles, to the trailhead, which is well marked and has a picnic table and outhouse. The trail is two miles and there are beautiful flowers in bloom; azaleas, iris, paintbrush, pitcher plant, Bolander's lily plus many others that I don't know. The trail is well maintained and not too strenuous.

We had a sheriff drive right to our door, checking on a forest fire at the Windy Valley trailhead. It had been reported by a passing motorist and luckily only burned two acres.

July 9 and 10 - Magic and Rianne B. and Laren and Jerrilynn W.; Gold Beach, OR

We're on the top of the world looking down on creation. The sunset last evening was exquisite! The only thing more exquisite was the herd of elk we saw last evening as we were scouting the area. We saw between seventeen and twenty (bulls and cows) and we got within thirty feet of them just down the road, as we rode on our motorcycles.

We hated to end the evening so we stayed up until 2:30 A.M. playing Canasta with the gorgeous half-moon shining in the window.

The view from the outhouse was inspiring! Thanks for directing our thoughts as we take care of business.

July 17 and 18 - Judi and Kurt C.; Auburn, WA, and Greg and Cindy E.; Bandon, OR

Perfect weather! Big flies! Great radio reception! The dogs loved the scents along the trail to Windy Valley.

The journal entries were entertaining. We had no sign of the rodents that others experienced up here.

The stars were incredible! The moonless night allowed great views of the Milky Way, a billion stars and every constellation.

We spent the evening playing Yahtzee and enjoying wine and beer.

Looks like we're catching the last of the rhododendrons and azaleas. Lots of Indian paint brush north of the lookout. White pine cone crop looks good this year.

July 19 and 20 - Bill and Karalei N.; Medford, OR, and John and Kris W.; Temecula, CA

This has indeed been an experience! There are seven of us in this place, none of us fond of hiking or any kind of strenuous exercise. The weather has cooperated and there have been no "trolls bowling on the roof," no killer

84

bolts of lightning and no bothersome bears. However there are three children under ten and this will compensate for the lack of the above. I do believe that this would have been an utterly sensational experience had we been childless.

We didn't see much wildlife at all. We had stocked up on several varieties of peanuts but only saw one baby chipmunk for a fleeting second. No "Timothy" the mouse either. We had plenty of beer and Kahlua left, so no elephants either...maybe next time when we come without the kids!

After a day and a half of fighting with the door knob, "Tim the Toolman Taylor" (a.k.a. Bill), removed it and lubricated it with dish detergent and it works perfectly now.

We told the kids, Timothy (10), Aaron (9) and Ashley (6) that they were really in for an "experience" before we came. We just didn't realize what kind of an "experience" the adults were in for. Like we said before, we would highly recommend leaving them at home next time so we could enjoy the peace and serenity of this solitude in God's country. It was a challenge to change clothes with two families sharing the 15' x 15' glass house. We also had to rearrange every single piece of furniture and item that wasn't bolted down to make room for sleeping.

All in all, it *truly* was an "experience" none of us will ever forget.

(Aaron, age 9) The first day we got here we flew our kites. We also found a huge rock for climbing. That night at six, my kite went up for about twenty minutes. We also had fun hurting my sister. We got crammed in the shack, and the trolls didn't fly off the roof, and the old outhouse had fallen over. Good luck!

July 24 - Roger and Donna S.; Gig Harbor, WA

Hi! We're back for our third year at the lookout. This time we left the boys with friends in Coos Bay and even though we're sorry *they* missed the experience, *we* loved being up here alone. Totally alone, completely alone, by ourselves!

It rained a lot Thursday and we were socked in by clouds and fog. Cool! Friday was beautiful but windy up here. We hiked down to Windy Valley and it was calm most of the way although we could hear the wind constantly howling above us. Everything smelled so fresh and clean after the rain. It was great!

July 26 - Richard and Miriam (10) K.; Rogue River, OR

As expected, the sights are magnificent...and the wind never stopped. No critters visiting at night...so sad for my daughter, as mice do "get her attention." I'm thankful my ears were saved from hearing loss.

A truly unique and wonderful experience for children. Stars abound, half-moon, extraordinary sunset last evening. So much to be thankful for. A good place to reflect on what is important.

July 27 - Bob, Evelyn, Jim (15) and Jeff (10) F.; Medford, OR

(Evelyn) Mid-afternoon. We arrived around 4 P.M. yesterday to my great relief. After running over a rock about ten miles from "camp" that sounded like it tore the bottom off the car, I had visions of being stranded in the wilderness! I guess the car was loaded more heavily than I thought! Anyway, I don't see any pools of fluid under the car today so maybe we'll even make it back home tomorrow.

The "hill" was quite intimidating upon first sight. Luckily we have two strong and helpful boys! The wheelbarrow really helped too! Next time we come we'll bring less "stuff" and more water. We haven't had to use the extra water left by a previous guest yet, as we're watching our usage carefully, but it's good to know it's there if we do need it.

It was a short night for me last night between the beautiful half-moon lighting up the place, the wind blowing like a hurricane and the gorgeous sunrise. I don't get up often enough to see these! Mother Nature commands your attention up here...it's an ever changing spectacle!

The kids and I took a hike to Snow Camp Meadow this morning and went kite flying. The wildflowers are beginning to fade but I did see one of those "orchids" that another guest mentioned earlier. The walk back up to the lookout was more exercise than I'm used to, but the bees, horseflies and kids a quarter mile ahead of me kept me plodding on! Nothing like kids to make you realize how old you're getting and keep you young at heart!

This afternoon we're napping, snacking and reading the journal entries. I'm glad we brought our kids...it's an experience everyone should have. It's great to be away from the phone, TV, doorbell, etc. My one concession is to let them listen to the Giants game on the radio tonight (die hard fans!). We haven't talked, laughed and played this much together in quite awhile...long overdue!

Thanks to the USFS for making this available and to all the previous "tenants" who have been taking such good care of it!

To those who come after us, we bequeath a kite and some extra toilet paper. No sign of Timothy...just a few ants.

We're off to the one-mile trail by Loeb Park. Supposed to be the largest grove of redwood trees in Oregon.

July 28 and 29 - Jim and Shirley M.; Grants Pass, OR

Wow! The ultimate cabin heater rises in the east. We relied on the little wood burner in the corner to warm us yesterday while the clouds claimed victory over the sun for the sky.

So many plant varieties on these slopes! Perhaps terrain and poor soil will spare peaks like this and others in the Kalmiopsis from being converted to tree farms. Politics and bad science cannot "manage" these slopes to higher productivity!

Thanks to the Siskiyou N.F. and volunteers for renovating and maintaining this fine hotel. Service is poor but the location and view are superb. There are also fine touches like the choice of horizontal or vertical outhouses…how thoughtful.

We were a bit discouraged yesterday…no porters to help with luggage, elevator out of service, etc.

We did camp out at Elko the night before arriving here. Great place but it is owned by mosquitoes.

Good road signing made it easy to find this site. Fortunately, the mindless sign slayers have not shot out all the road signs as they have done in other areas. Seeing the road gate punctured by armor-piercing bullets is a bit disturbing. Boys and their toys!

July 29 and 30 - Doug, Linda, Brian and Leslie S.; Cave Junction, OR

(Leslie, age 14) Hello, my fellow adventurers! Unlike others, we only had to make one trip up that hill with our stuff. My dad pushed the small wheelbarrow up the hill (it got a break for once). The other three of us were "loaded" down with much, much more. After taking twenty minutes to get up here and slightly organize our stuff, we began to relax and played a game of Yahtzee. I won and my dad lost dreadfully. He was as unlucky as a flea getting hit by a bolt of lightning!

I love the 360 degree view from inside. I would love to have a house with windows all around. Although you would have to clean the windows often, it would be worth it.

The sunset last night was gorgeous. It reminded me of a painting I had seen once. It was of the sun coming up from behind the earth; it appeared as if the earth was on fire. It was titled "SunRise." (There is meaning in the way the title is written.) Nature imitates art.

Sitting up here looking around, you can appreciate life, not only your own but the earth's. OK, stand up, go outside, walk around the deck at least once if you have not done it yet. Now think of how many generations, centuries, millenniums have gone by. We have only been here a fraction (1 billion) of what we even know of. Humans cannot destroy the earth, we can only destroy ourselves. The earth is not a new creation but a "life (as we know it) sustaining object" floating in space, and after we are gone it will be again. Sorry about the lecture but I'm the kind of person who likes others to hear my point of view. Oops, probably not the place to do it. Something to think about, though.

Last night I was awake most of the night listening to a frog and a cricket have a conversation. They went on for hours.

The firefinder in the middle of the room is fun to play with. The only problem is that the window pane is often in the way of your viewing.

We are also going to see the ocean and run in the foam. My dog loves the ocean...he is afraid of the edge though...he jumps over the edge of the water.

We'll be back. Bye you all. Have fun.

P.S. We left a *National Geographic* magazine here. It is on lightning. It is especially neat'o when you are staying "up here."

Oh, and for the man who wrote that he only ate bananas and eggs, we left a can of Italian tomatoes and a package of chicken soup.

August 1, 2 and 3 - Beth and Kurt; Central Point, OR

(August 3, 6:20 A.M. - Kurt) In a few hours we will be leaving. I thought Beth would have written a book by now, but she has gone back to sleep after seeing the sunrise. So it's up to me to bring our journal entry up to date.

We arrived at approximately 2 P.M. on the first after staying a night in Packers Cabin* southeast of here. Wind was blowing hard and continued blowing very hard until about noon on August 2nd. It felt like the lookout was going to topple off its foundation the first night. We awoke this A.M. at 5:30 to see the sky afire until 6:08, when the sunball made its appearance. We noticed how quiet it is this morning, no wind, not even a breeze. Eerie!!

Woke up around 7:30, missed the sunrise. We ate breakfast and did some house cleaning. Beth is drawing some posters for her first grade classroom. I started reading last year's journal after August 6, the day we were here. I must report that "Timothy" is alive, as he left his calling card(s). Too noisy last night to hear him. I fell asleep reading the journal on the bed. Woke up at 1:30 P.M., a three hour nap! Only up here could I do that and not feel guilty. Beth was sunbathing on the picnic table when I awoke. We each showered, those solar showers work great. We packed lunch after killing all the flies. They don't seem to come in the open windows, but do find the door. All were left open to keep the lookout as cool as possible.

Our picnic was at Game Lake. When we arrived a FS vehicle was there. We chose a site to place our blanket and eat. After wandering around checking things out, we arrived back at the truck and noticed we had a flat tire. It appeared a sharp rock punctured the sidewall. Game Lake is small, just a few acres, and shallow. Water was warm.

(Beth) This morning, Kurt took a few crumbs out behind the lookout to where he had left our leftover eggs yesterday. A little chipmunk was sitting there just waiting for today's breakfast special. We were pleased to see that "Timothy" (or relative) was alive and well. In fact, he came out on the counter while we were sitting at the table playing cribbage. We are not sure if he came through the open window or was behind the counter. He did leave his calling cards the previous night but again the window had been open.

Kurt finally did win that game of cribbage (the first in a year), but only because I was a little worried that "Timothy" would run across my feet. It's hard to play a whole game with your feet in the chair! But it's all part of the great experience.

Next year we'll have to stay a week. To those who are lucky enough to follow, enjoy! And hope for a breeze in this heat.

One final note, last year we were just starting to get to know each other. In July of this year we became engaged. By this time next year, we will be married and return to celebrate.

Author's Note: Packers Cabin and Ludlum House are two other places available to rent from the USFS through the Chetco Ranger District. Both are within one hour's drive of Brookings. Reservations can be made by contacting the Chetco Ranger District, 555 Fifth Street, Brookings, Oregon 97415, (541) 469-2196. Current rate is $20 per night.

August 5 and 6 - Joe and Judy S.; Shady Cove, OR

Arrived about 12:30 P.M. Surprised to see the last renters still here. Joe was just as surprised to learn that he knew one of the renters. I guess it reminds us that "it's a small world." This is a part of the world we could spend the summer at. What an indescribably wonderful view. This will be a beautiful memory of celebrating our anniversary. By the way, congratulations to the last renters on setting "the date." Maybe we'll cross paths again up here.

Had a wonderfully peaceful rest and cozy dinner. Then about 7 P.M. we got a wild hare to set off due northwest "as the buzzard flies" for Snow Camp Meadow. It was about seventy-six degrees, beautiful sunny sky. After walking, falling, crawling and flying over brush tops, we arrived, thirty minutes later, at the most picturesque meadow. After a hike and a quick glimpse of a deer, we discovered the trail back up to Windy Valley. All in all, an insightful adventure. We had to hurry back in time to take a picture of the spectacular sunset, for we remembered the binoculars and forgot the camera.

We had a visit from "Timothy." After several grabs for the flashlight, we caught him full checked, stealing our toilet paper. We persuaded him to exit the nearest window. Aah, peaceful sleep at last…not. Whoever thought a clock could tick so loud. The wind started to pick up about 11:30, blowing from the east, drastic drop in temperature. It's fun to experience a lot of weather in so short a stay. I'm having a blast.

Woke to a brilliant orange and pink sky, with just a thin band of clouds over mountain tops. I hope my camera captures even a tenth of the beauty. It's about sixty-three degrees, wind still clipping right along, 40 to 50 mph. I love that sound.

Finished reading most of journals, what a neat way to get a feel for this country.

August 6, 7 and 8 - Steve W. and Gilbert K.; Troutdale and Dayton, OR

(Steve) Wrapping up another successful expedition to yet one more great lookout. The three of us had high spirits for the duration, going by the count of dead flies by late afternoon. I took some video of sunsets, one was time lapse. As usual, I made use of solar power extensively, two water heaters and two electric panels for electronic cooler.

August 9 - Judy F. and Brad E.; Brookings, OR

Needless to say…we're here and you're not! All the better!! One twenty-four hour stay is not long enough. Now we've got to go back and deal with life as we now live it.

Slept very well…probably because of the three mile hike to Windy Valley. Took lots of video and pictures to remember this totally awesome visit.

While I'm writing this, Brad has packed up and cleaned up…he does such fine work. So I better get my buns moving.

We'll be back! Oh, and I found the "O" to someone's Scrabble game.

August 9, 10 and 11 - Randy, Janice and David; Clatskanie, OR

(Janice) We arrived here at lookout on Monday after having spent four nights at Packer's Cabin. Before we came here, spent one night in Brookings where we found a hot shower, a firm bed and electricity! We've been rough-ing it since we left home so a hot shower was wonderful. Plan to stay here two nights.

Most everything I've read in this journal sums up what I would say about the lookout. It's been a wonderful experience and could have been more peaceful if we hadn't had our nine year old son! He's too active for us but I'm glad he has been here to enjoy our adventures and share our great memories.

(August 11) After getting back from our hike yesterday, the fog rolled in about 2 P.M. and stayed the rest of the afternoon and night. We really felt closed in from the whole world.

I'm writing this the day we're leaving at 6 A.M. The fog has lifted but the wind is still blowing very, very hard. I had mentioned that I'd like a house built here but now I've changed my mind. My only concern at this moment is getting safely off this hill without losing our gear and ourselves.

By the way, "Timothy" is still here! My husband got the munchies last night about midnight while he was trying to cool down the cabin. He had the window open and "Timothy" (at least that's who we think it was), jumped up on the window sill to say "Hi...."

I don't know who jumped the highest, him or my husband!

Well, so long for now! Enjoy and make some memories!

August 11 and 12 - The McGrath family; Portland, OR

A boulder damaged the step on the motor home and **someone** said they would pick next year's exciting adventure! Good thing we brought two strong teenage boys to use the wheelbarrow.

When the wind is not blowing, it is so quiet we automatically whisper. Really can see the ocean!

The night of the 11th, we saw at least two dozen shooting stars. Still falling at 2 A.M. on the 12th.

(August 12) Hiked to Snow Camp Meadow. Nice. Checked out the Darlingtonias by the streams.

Someone plans to come back minus the motor home.

By the way, this group did not unglue the chair, we are all lightweights.

All the previous writers seemed younger. We are grandparents, the parents of our charges are too old to camp and hike.

August 13 - Bartles; Salem, OR

We rode the Hellgate Jet Boat on Thursday and then drove through the redwoods before coming up here.

We had two visitors from Germany. We were surprised to see them way up here. They had taken the road from Gold Beach. They were interested to know we could rent places like this. Limited vocabulary on both parts but fun to share what we could. The sunset was a disappointment, not much color.

"Timothy" made an early visit at 4:15 A.M. He scampered up the stairs, ran around the deck and peeked in the windows as he did gymnastics on the frames.

Last but not least is the best outhouse (w.c.) on the west coast. Here is a spectacular view where one can take it all in **and** let it all out!

August 19, 20 and 21 - Paul and Wanda C.; Grants Pass, OR

Arrived Thursday afternoon to fog and drizzle and it is very windy. You don't realize how much you can do without when you have to make four trips up **that** hill. After the second one, Paul decided to use the wheelbarrow!

(August 20, 7 A.M.) Fogged in and rain. Decided to go to the meadow anyway, didn't notice the sign (which is located at the bottom of *that* hill), so we walked about six miles on the various roads, got back and while yours truly was in the outhouse, Paul shouts "I found it!" About ten yards down the Windy Valley trail, a sign also states Snow Camp Meadow! So after another two miles, we found the meadow. No elk but lots of rifle fire. Some idiot was practicing and scaring them all off!

Everywhere we went it was clear. Got back, heavy fog and rain. Still very peaceful and did enjoy not having to answer the phone or mow the lawn, etc., etc.

Leaving now, Saturday A.M. Clear skies, warm...figures.

August 21, 22, 23 and 24 - Joan and Larry; Eugene, OR

Arrived Saturday to a still, sunny, warm day, not a cloud in the sky or even a breeze. No bugs or mice either. It's our second visit of the season. After settling in, we went looking for Panther Lake, a phantom for sure. Nice drive.

(Monday) Drove down to Loeb State Park for a short hike through old growth redwood forest. It was cloudy and starting to get windy at the lookout but was sunny and warm down below. The wind gradually picked up all evening and was *howling* by the time we went to bed. We had been hoping to experience the wind that others reported and we did! Wondered all night how we'd ever get down the hill with all our stuff and fully expected the wheelbarrow to be in Brookings by morning.

We had great food, great music, great wine and great company (just us). Enjoyed it all. We plan to seek out other lookouts as someone mentioned earlier in the journal. Larry could spend a whole summer at a lookout, enjoying the beautiful scenery, peace and quiet. We'll be back!

August 26, 27 and 28 - John and Chad T.; Monmouth, OR

We arrived at about 6 P.M. after having to change a tire on our Explorer at the bottom of the hill. Chad worked the jack, no easy task, while I got the spare. Since we had driven on the flat for about five miles, it was pretty chewed up.

When we arrived at the lookout, two radio technicians from the Rogue River National Forest in Medford were working on the radio tower outside. The wind was blowing and one of them was up working on the tower itself. The fellow on the ground said they were installing a new repeater and taking the other one back to Medford to be used on their forest. As I talked to the one working in the building about hiking up by Game Lake, he stated that it was one of the base camps for the Silver Fire five years ago. He had been dropped by helicopter here at Snow Camp to set up special radio equipment on the peak just north of the lookout. Anyway, he said that one morning at Game Lake, he spotted an elk standing in the lake eating some algae.

When we entered the lookout, I could already tell there were many upgrades since our last visit two years ago. With the new floor, I guess there is no way the mouse can enter or leave as he/she desires. Thanks for the amenities.

The wind really blew tonight and with the drafty window on the east, we built a fire. That really helped. Thanks for the bounty of firewood so close by. My wife and I stayed at Acker Rock Lookout and had to carry in our own firewood, up the half mile trail to the lookout.

(August 27) We didn't get to Snow Camp Meadow on our last visit, so thanks to the directions from previous tenants this year, we found the trailhead off of the Windy Valley trail. Seeing the meadow up close was a treat.

We also made driving trips to Wild Horse and Quail Prairie lookouts. Both on forty foot towers and the view from each is worth seeing. Both lookouts were very accommodating and took time to show us different landmarks we asked about.

September 12 - Don and Viv (newlyweds); Chicago, IL

What a wild place for a honeymoon. We were only able to reserve one day. But what a day! On the way up, we saw no one except the occasional herd of Sasquatch. I kept bracing for a logging truck to bear down on us around the next turn. The road gave our rent-a-car a workout.

It's been very windy all day, getting even worse after sunset. The wind is howling and buffeting the lookout as I write. They remind me of stories my Irish mother told us about the eerie howling and screeching of the wind along the rugged northwest coast of Donegal. Our imaginations run wild with the weird sounds of the high winds.

The sunset was awesome. Not a cloud in the sky. We watched the shadows creep along the hills. The sun gradually dipped into the Pacific and disappeared, leaving a reddish-orange glow to outline the horizon and to mark its passing. We watched this out on the deck until the howling wind's bitter chill forced us into the warm interior with its wood burning stove and a pot of bubbling hot chili.

Later the stars gradually started to appear (boy, the wind is blowing now), along with the lights of Brookings or Crescent City in the far off distance.

Well, I gotta go now, my fine young bride is calling me to bed.

September 18 and 19 - Larry and Joanne; Talent, OR

What a place with a view. Another one of God's better ideas.

September 19, 20 and 21 - Jeff and Kim P; Medford, OR

Year two...we're back!! Back for more! Couldn't get enough time last year in August (only one day). The furniture has been rearranged. I like this better. As for the demise of "Timothy"...I know not. (Read last year's journal, August 17).

Toto reconfirmed my suspicions that we were not in Kansas nor Oregon!! The winds last night could've easily had up to 100 mph gusts. There was quite a windstorm! It felt like we were going to take off. I was a bit in panic when I stepped outside and then couldn't find the door. It was dark and I didn't have my flashlight. I'm glad that everything is bolted down well! Outhouse included!

We hiked to Snow Camp Meadow...a definite must! Check out the water closely. There are mud puppies! Something I haven't seen in years. They are cute.

Oh...there seems to be an ant problem!

(September 21) We're working on little sleeps this Tuesday A.M. We stayed awake listening to information about the two earthquakes near Klamath Falls. It sounds bad.

Well, it's home to Medford now to see if our home felt the quake. We'll be back!

P.S. Sorry, but we weren't the "bad guys," the two bolts/nuts that are missing from the wheelbarrow were gone when we got here. The weight of everything going up (gravity) to the lookout works fine. It doesn't going down. Gravity is a bit different coming down. Yeah, it's the same gravity, just working at a different advantage. (Signed: Dr. Science)

September 22 - Dennis, Gabe and Elijah A.; Applegate, OR

In spite of what seemed to be an early start, we finally arrived here last evening shortly before sunset. We treated ourselves to the first break of the day as we silently watched the colorful sun dip into the ocean.

After a couple more trips to and from the rig, we finally had much more supplies than we needed! But, with two strong, energetic teenage sons, why not? With Gabe (16) and Elijah (13), FOOD was the main load and the most spoken word of the evening. Sometime between meals last night, we managed to break out our guitars and compete with the howling winds. (When it comes to "punk" and "heavy metal," I'll give it a "7.6", but you can't dance to it!) It was getting late when we turned out our Coleman lantern and broke out the binoculars. The lights of Brookings, Crescent City, Gold Beach, ships, stars, half-moon…they were all in attendance.

The night was windy but cozy…of course, being the oldest and wisest of the bunch, I got the bed. (Actually, I used guilt and power-played 'em.) Young people can handle hard, cold floors.

Venus, the morning star, was the first thing I saw in the eastern sky at 5:45 this morning. I built a small fire to rid the morning chill before waking my camp buddies. They wouldn't budge. The sun peeked over Pearsoll Peak at 7:06 A.M. and began to color the stretch of hills, working its way to the faint Pacific on the horizon. Gabe and Elijah managed to each take a glimpse through one eye, before going back to sleep.

Meanwhile, I read just about everything in here from *The Osborne Fire Finder* manual to *Port Orford Cedar Root Disease* before I came to the journal. I loved it! My chuckling even woke the boys. We spent a couple of hours enjoying the descriptions and experiences of others. Kinda adds a nice chunk to ours.

We have had no ants, mice or any other intruders that we read about in the journal. (Is it us?) Just wind, wind and wind.

I want to thank my friend David for this opportunity to be here. Without his love, concern and generosity, this experience would not have been a part of our wonderful memories. Memories in the making. Thank you David. Thank you Snow Camp. Thank you USFS. Thank you Gabe and Elijah. Thank you Creator. Aloha.

P.S. Have fun, David and Barbara. May you experience the spirit of "Timothy" and survivors…and David, leave that solar panel alone!!

September 23 and 24 - "Ranger" D.C. (David) and "Ranger" B.K. (Barbara); Applegate and Grants Pass, OR

(David - September 24) Day two, we leave tomorrow, boo hoo!

Thank you! Thank you! Thanks for so many things. Isn't life grand….

Took a hike today on Tin Cup Trail, about ten road miles away. Hiked five hard hours so we'll sleep soundly tonight. Saw a mama bear and her cub. They never knew we were there so we had two to three minutes of wonder.

Even treated ourselves to a somewhat warm solar shower just as the sun faded away. Definitely one of the fastest showers of my life.

The "Mr. Fixit" side of me will attempt to repair the wheelbarrow tomorrow. I'm hoping the spare bolts in my truck will do the job.

A pause to eat a delicious supper. When the attractive cook was asked what kind of Mexican dish it was, she said, "I don't know." Whatever…it was great.

The weather has been warm in the days, windy up here. Didn't need much of a fire last night.

The half-moon seen with a spotting scope is worth every dollar of the lookout rental, not to mention all the other stuff.

My coffee and sodas all taste better here. I like this glass house. We will return.

We promised ourselves to wake up long enough to see the sunrise tomorrow morning.

(Barbara) And thank you, David, for having the idea in the first place and for sharing this experience with me. As always, our time together was delightful. The weather, including every single gust of wind, the spectacular view, the ocean, crashing waves from this vantage point was my favorite, if one could have a favorite view from here on top of the world.

And now some comic relief. We've had our second group of company: Harrell's Septic has arrived, and I thought we could escape all the modern conveniences of city living this far away. Oh well….

Up to the wee hours of this morning, I was beginning to think this "Infamous Timothy" legend was a myth and I found myself a little disappointed at not being able to see the "Great Timothy," and low and behold, he woke me up with a bit of a scare tapping on the east window. I feel honored…somewhat!

I'll always remember this great time…seeing the mother and baby bear was very, very special. Two days go too fast when you're having so much fun. Hopefully, we'll be back next year.

(David) Barbara, I love you so much. It is times like this that my heart feels like it could burst with joy. I'm so glad you came into my life.

September 27 - Scott, Lisa and Norah; Lake Oswego, OR

Funny how some people feel this is a great place to bring the kids while others vow to leave them at home next time. Our story is different. We brought Norah, our three month old baby girl to Snow Camp to celebrate *her conception here a year ago* (see September 31, 1992)! Yep, she's a Snow Camp production, her ethereal spirit; a hum in the beauty of these craggy mountains noticed our play and selected us as parents for a tour of the mortal side. So you see we *found* her here…of course we'll always bring her back.

If you've read the 1992 entry, you'll understand that there wasn't a lot of choice in amusements due to driving wind and rain. This year we've been impressed by the view, sunsets, sunrises, etc., but have decided that cold and rainy is preferable to hot and arid. It's easier by far to keep warm (as I've already mentioned), than to keep cool.

We are delighted to have had two nights instead of one but the cooler ice is meltwater and general campcraft is less delightful in the searing sun. We greatly miss having a fire in the woodstove. Who'd have thought it'd be swearing high eighties at us at 4,000 plus feet in almost October? We can't understand how it doesn't even get cool at *night*. Totally clear skies in the mountains.

Norah? Oh, she loves it here. We've taken her camping almost every weekend since she was six weeks old. This is the Ritz compared to tenting up the Lostine River in the Wallowas! She seems quite at home in the wilderness as well she should. Right now she is on my lap enthusiastically gumming my left thumb…an early teether.

Oh, we considered naming Norah something pertaining to her origins, but didn't in the end. I talked to an expert on Oregon's Native American cultures (historical) who reported that there is no record of the language of this area's indigenous peoples. Apparently a graduate student couldn't negotiate or afford to pay the last person alive who spoke the language (years ago) to record it, and that person died, taking an entire language with him. Alas, we were hoping for some melodic translation of "storm" or "snow" or "mountaintop" or "wind" or "camp"… kinda goofy but neat, too.

September 28 - D.M. and C.B.; Talent, OR, and M.B. and B.W.; Augsburg, Germany

We had a somewhat unusual welcoming committee here; we found a U.S. Army helicopter parked in the front yard! Actually, it was the Forest Service repairing the radio.

It was a beautiful bright night, as we watched the fog creeping up the valley. We placed bets on whether it would reach us or not. It didn't. The moonlight was lovely, but it did hamper our stargazing which was a pity because we had quite the hobby astronomer here from Germany.

We roasted last night in our down sleeping bags. Who would have thought it would be warm way up here, the end of September?

Wonderful sunrise, with an amazingly bright Venus directly above Big Craggies. Quite the experience for us coming from "downtown" Talent (population 3,200) and for our visiting relatives from Germany.

Falls hier noch andere aus Deutschland sind: Viele Grüsse!!! Hier kann man meinen, man steht auf dem Gipfel der Welt!!!

September 30, October 1, 2 and 3 - Wayne and Carol; Medford, OR

We successfully flew our kite this time and it didn't end up on the roof. We're getting better. Till next year....

October 5, 6, 7 and 8 - Gene and Joy-Ann J. with "Kisher Jane, the Original Wonder Cat;" Colusa, CA

Have to tell you how we met "Timothy." We were here in August 1990 and brought our camping cat, Catfish. Well, a little after dark, Catfish came in with a little mouse and let it loose in here. The little guy wasn't hurt, but he did have the interesting "trademark" of getting up in the window sill and doing his thing from pane to pane. That's how Gene was able to gently catch him in a T-shirt and show him to the door. Makes me wonder if that's how he originally came to be a lookout house mouse. Someone the cat drug in.

"Timothy" scared Kisher Jane (cat); she has been under the blankets the whole time up here! Guess he's (Timothy) getting even!

October 9 - Amber, Lindsey, Tate, Amy, Ty and Dads; Gold Beach, OR

Our stay here has been wonderful and the weather was great! I slept out on the deck last night and there must've been a million stars. This morning we woke up at about 5:30 A.M. and us "kids" stayed up until about 6:30 A.M. when we finally talked the "dads" into letting us go hunting. We saw three does, no bucks and a beautiful sunrise. We had fun exploring, and Tate even saw a raccoon! The heavy brush was great for fort making. Amber (9), Lindsey (4), Tate (11), Amy (12) and Ty (13) had fun shooting the BB gun and sling shots.

Right now I'm sitting on the tipped over outhouse and have a beautiful view of the ocean, Brookings, the road and forests! The ocean is especially neat as are the ever changing clouds. This is only my opinion, but this was really cool!

As I sit here on the sideways outhouse, I look over a sea of evergreens, speckled with clearcut and crisscrossed with roads.

Today I went on an exploring expedition. We explored the south side of the ridge which was very thick with underbrush and very easy to get lost in. The view from here is very inspiring and I've had a wonderful time. I hope that anyone else who comes here enjoys the beautiful surroundings and weather and doesn't destroy the forts we've built!

As we prepare to leave, my mom is scraping dog crap off the balcony. I saw Bigfoot yesterday and I said, "Yo, Bigfoot, how's your Hollywood honey doin'?" He said, "Peace, brother!"

My name is Tate and we're here with our friends. I'm from Jamaica and I have big dread locks and I sing a lot and I'm crazy and I have to go now! I'm sitting in the outhouse and the smell and view is very funky in here! Aaah, it's tipping over on me! I now have chimichonga on my leg! I gotta go clean up now! Peace, man!

October 10 - Steve and Deborah; Arcata, CA

Came to celebrate my forty-eighth birthday and what an excellent choice. Weather OK with a few showers. Ironic, since it appears this is the latest in the season the lookout has been used for years. No sign of the mysterious "Timothy." Perhaps he's hibernating already or afraid of our dog…with no reason. How about a composting toilet when this one fills up (next week)?

October 14 - J.P.D.

Snow Camp has my nomination as the recreational facility with the best view from a vault toilet.　　AMEN!

That was the last entry for Snow Camp's 1993 season.

AUTHOR DEMONSTRATES
PROPER TECHNIQUE FOR CONQUERING "THE HILL."

"Are the four wheel drive hubs in?"

RULE BENDING

September 22, 1993

With sweat dripping off my brow and soaking my T-shirt, my face pointing at the rough rocky road, I'm beginning to think that the rule surely wouldn't apply to me, especially if I didn't get caught. My mind started reeling off the excuses I could use if I did get caught. What would be the worst thing they could do to me? Would I be talking to someone who would understand my "good ol' country boy logic?"

The morning had started off well with no real hassles up till now. I had left the house in my trusty 1962 Ford 4x4 pickup truck (rebuilt so many times you could call it new), at close to the time I'd set for myself. The back was loaded with everything we would need and some things that we didn't. But that was just par for me. Call me "Mr. Prepared."

My truck was always burdened with everything I thought a person might need in case of an emergency. Besides the "standard" items such as a PTO winch, tire chains, ax, two shovels, hydraulic jack, hi-lift jack, flares, first aid kit, ropes, bungee straps, tow chains, jumper cables, tools, flashlight, spotlight, gloves, many maps, sunglasses, repair manual, spare parts (points, distributor cap, etc.), you'll also find coveralls, a coat, long johns, cookies in a Tupperware container and a roll of toilet paper for those *true* emergencies. My friends think I drive around in my truck just praying for something to happen so I will have a reason to use my "emergency equipment" and prove I'm not neurotic after all.

I left my house around 9 A.M. with the promise of a nice sunny day ahead. Drove to Grants Pass to pick up Barbara at her house. As I packed most of the camping equipment, she only had a few things to throw in besides the groceries she picked up to add to the two ice chests. Juggling the contents of the ice chests and cargo boxes takes more time than I wanted to allow so Barbara's patience came through again by calming this frustrated man's emotions with her soothing demeanor. A few more last minute things that just have to be done

101

and we are on our way. Anyone looking at the back of this full-size pickup, would think we were camping for two weeks, not two days.

The road west into the Coastal Mountains from Merlin is paved but narrow and very winding. You leave the Rogue River to go over the mountains and join it again on the other side about twenty miles from the sea and the town of Gold Beach. It has a fair amount of traffic due to people shuttling cars and rafts back from their trips down the Wild and Scenic Rogue River. As these are young mountains, the terrain is very steep. Whether driving or riding, looking over the side of this road will make most travelers want to end this segment of their trip quickly. A hair-raising experience to say the least. Barbara's patience wears a little thin in this stretch.

With a deep sigh of relief, we rejoined the Rogue River again on the ocean side, and were happy to have about ten miles of relatively flat but winding paved road along the river (a little cooler now due to the ocean air reaching inland). Then we turned south heading back in to the mountains toward Snow Camp; this road is winding and steep with a gravel surface. Less traffic is offset by a loose surface that allows your vehicle to lose traction on any corner you might take too fast. Barbara's patience is marvelous and I slow down in consideration of her fears (and mine). Meeting a fully loaded logging truck on one of those corners takes something out of you.

A half mile short of the lookout, we encountered the locked gate. The combination the Forest Service gave us to the lock is the right one so we must be in the right place. Locking the gate behind us gives me my first taste of Snow Camp's flavor. I like my privacy so the gate is just my cup of tea (strike that and make it coffee, with half-and-half). It is on this last stretch of very bumpy road that we get the first sighting of our destination. Yep, it's a lookout all right.

From the parking lot at the bottom of the hill, I see that the last 200 yards of road is steep, rugged, out-sloped and generally treacherous. Just my cup of coffee! But the Forest Service brochure said "Do not attempt to drive the last 200 yards to the lookout." Obviously not a road for a "flatlander's" two-wheel drive vehicle, but probably a piece of cake for my trusty truck. I spot a red wheelbarrow at the base of the hill, but "have fun" isn't written all over it. I estimate that to get everything from the back of the truck to the top of the hill is about seven wheelbarrow trips. Did I mention that I'm over forty? I'm also a bit of the macho type, which means I'd have to push the wheelbarrow at least four of the seven trips. Barbara is going to figure out pretty soon just what kind of shape I'm in. The first anniversary since we met was fast approaching and I created a decent illusion up until now. This wheelbarrow business could blow my cover. Stalling for time, I suggested we carry a light load up to the lookout to assess the situation and look at the view.

The day is hot and it is mid-afternoon, so half way up the hill, reasons for *bending the rule* are flooding my mind. Upon reaching the summit, Snow Camp Lookout presents itself. The climb was wiped from our minds as we beheld the breathtaking view. The piercing blue sky hovers over an incredible range of purple mountains, green valleys, tiny roads, and large clearcuts until it blends into the blue of the Pacific Ocean as far as the eye can see. The first impression is marred a wee bit by a fiberglass module "building" that holds radio equipment and a slender tower standing in front and to the right of the lookout. I see two large photovoltaic panels on the radio house, for supplying power to the batteries and the radio system. I admire them quietly making electricity with no moving parts. Otherwise, it is a grand little glass building with a simply spectacular view. It is difficult to take my eyes off the surrounding vista long enough to assess why I shouldn't bring the truck up here (other than the fact that the brochure said not to).

The combination to the gate lock works on the lock to the lookout door also. With the sun shining in from the west and since the windows were closed, the inside is stifling. We open the four windows, one centered on each side, and look at the view from the outside catwalk until the lookout cools down a little. Never can I recall being this high up and having such a 360 degree view. To the west lies the Pacific Ocean. You can look right down Pistol River to the ocean where huge rocks sit in the sea near the beach. To the south, I suspect I can see beyond the California-Oregon border. To the east, I am looking into and beyond the Kalmiopsis Wilderness area. The Big Craggies Botanical Area is comprised of some huge cliffs in the wilderness area that stare back at us. "Simply awesome," my son would say.

As I ventured back inside the lookout, Tom Bodett's soothing voice (he does the radio commercials for Motel 6), kept sounding in my head. "No wake up calls, loud neighbors, bad art, ice machine, maid service, or tipping. It's about as far away from the freeway as you can get, checkout time is noon, and all this for only $30 a night. Why, you can't beat that with a stick...."

But no more stalling. I either have to start packing or pushing (the wheelbarrow), or drive the truck up here. The "parking lot" at the top is small but there is room to turn around and even room for another vehicle if necessary. But there is no way I can "hide" the truck while it is up here. It is so exposed that any Forest Service employee on any of the surrounding roads could spot it in a minute. It would be like trying to hide a wart on the end of your nose. If you can't hide, then do it with pride.

OK, decision is made, put the hubs in, drive the truck up here, unload everything quickly and move the truck back to the lower parking lot. That means only one more trip down and back today on foot power, both with no load. I can handle that...I'll exercise tomorrow. Now, I have to get this idea past Barbara (my conscience). I do get it past her, but there is no way she will ride with me. OK again, as she'll probably leave fingerprints permanently embossed in the dash board.

All that is done in a flash and the truck again sits in the lower parking lot, stripped bare — empty enough to hold a dance in the back. Scattered about, in and out of the lookout, are all the items I packed, some needed and some not. I didn't need to bring the cooking utensils as there are plenty here already. I see other things that are duplicated but "what the hey," I didn't have to pack it up that hill. And we now have "plenty" of water, maybe ten gallons, plus the solar shower which is full. Early tomorrow I'll put it in the sun so as to have hot water for a shower in the evening.

Now is the time to settle in and relax. Like so many vacations, it has taken a lot of energy to get here but there is no doubt, it was well worth it. Sunset is near at hand and the sky is vivid with colors. Barbara, being the artist, is allowing me to see all the beauty which surrounds us through her more appreciative eyes. Beauty is multidimensional and can be found in the simplest of things. It is all part of learning to slow down and really enjoy life. Nothing epitomizes that concept more than Snow Camp Lookout.

As we discussed plans for hiking through the Kalmiopsis Wilderness, my eyes fell upon a book, a loose-leaf binder labeled "Snow Camp Journal." Barbara and I could barely contain our excitement as we snuggled up by the light of the moon and prepared to read...

..."June 16, 1990 - Gary and Kathy P.; Brookings, OR"

"I don't do windows."

SNOW CAMP JOURNAL — 1994

June 2, 3 and 4 - Gary D.; Wedderburn, OR

The first order of business is to put out "Old Glory."

And away we go. The 1994 season at Snow Camp lookout has started. Two more trips up the hill just about did me in. It was time to rest. Little or no wind. It was warm and sunny. Time to "shuck down," get the jug of sour mash and catch some rays.

So what does a man alone do for two days on a mountaintop? He enjoys the sun when possible, he reads *(Central Point PC Tools for Windows)*, he has a few drinks and enjoys the beauty that surrounds him.

The old Pro 34 never had it so good. That's a Radio Shack scanner. Excellent radio reception.

(June 4 - 6:30 A.M.) Fogged in on all sides. Much rain and wind last night. NOTE: Several of the windows leak on the south end of the cabin! The foam pad got soggy last night. I'll call the ranger district this afternoon.

Took some of the gear down to the car. Surprise! Surprise! One very flat tire. Will attempt to put this "donut" on. This may possibly be a problem. If it can't be done, it's going to be a long drive back to Gold Beach.

June 4 - Tracy and Morgan; Brookings, OR

(Tracy) We passed a Probe headed for Gold Beach with a flat tire. Seems to have been the former tenant. He didn't want to use our lug wrench.

We saw a herd of elk in Fairview Meadow. They would not stop for the camera, however.

The quiet has a calming effect after living with traffic noise for so long. True, Brookings is not as stressful as San Francisco, but nothing beats a wilderness mountaintop for recreating.

My son, Morgan (17), went to check the outhouse on top because I asked him to. He came back with a bad report which I found difficult to believe. He had scouted the 1958 version, thank goodness, and the modern one is firmly planted.

I scouted out the trail we plan to take in the morning with our dog, Bert,

who loves the outdoors but doesn't like the linoleum floor of the lookout.
It doesn't give him firm footing. He's old and deaf, but beautiful and loyal
I brought up the throw from the car for him to walk around on.

The setting sun has turned the sea into molten lava.

(June 5 - 9:15 A.M.) It's forty-four degrees on the thermometer and
the wind, although relatively mild, sounds very close to a "crashing surf."
Maybe this explains the journal references.

The sun falls
All around the mounted temple.
Across the horizon, dazzling colors are airbrushed.
Clouds are coming alive.
They slowly shuffle through the trees, lurking until
They reach the threshold of leaping forward.
Close the eyes and behold
A magnificent creation lurking below the foothill of this mounted
temple.   Morgan.

June 9 - Ryan, Paul, Rachel, Anne, Correy, Mike, Cathy, Eric, Paige and Melissa; Eugene, OR

Ten extremely stoked students from the Oregon Institute of Marine
Biology (OIMB) stayed here last night. Saw a beautiful sunset and a beautiful sunrise. We smoked some, we drank some, we ate some and generally
had a wonderful experience.

Yesterday we hiked to, and swam at, Vulcan Lake. Worth the three mile
round-trip hike. The stream flowing out of it was one of the most beautiful
I've ever seen. We also saw three bears on the drive here.

I must say the crapper here has the best view of any portable potti I've
had the pleasure of using. A most majestic dump!

(Anne M.) With the dying glow of the sunset still in my mind's eye, I
awoke to the sweet tones of a sunrise over mountains deeply textured in
blue...more shades of blue in that depth than I've ever seen. What a sweet
place. I can't wait to come back for more sweet weather and perhaps a storm!

The cabin was awesome...the bed was much too small though for ten
people.

(Melissa G.) I have spent the last three months at the OIMB, along with
the rest of my fellow comrades. These past months have been a learning and
growing experience and now I could ask for no better way to end my time in
Oregon. I'll be going back to California but who knows, I may end up in
Eugene in the fall.

My cup of coffee never tasted so good.

June 10 and 11 - Marcy and Kent; Eureka, CA

(Saturday, 8 A.M.) Finally out of bed for coffee. "The only thing wrong with this place," says Kent, "is deciding where to look next." Subtle sunrise, it's as if the sunset colors crept over the mountains to glow again with the sunrise...magenta and a luminous yellow I've never been able to describe.

We're pretty tired this morning because we were up so many times in the night, waking each other to see stars, Milky Way, fog settling in the valley and sunrise. This place is like the original full-screen drive-in!! Funny how when one has depleted analogies, we turn to descriptions of technology.

The wind was a continuous song all night. Too warm to need a fire. It's sixty-eight degrees...promise of a hot one today.

Oh, I have to tell about the fawn on the drive up. Doe and new fawn on the gravel road...we came around the corner...no time for baby to run...fawn dropped to a flattened crouch (looking a lot like a large quail), and froze on the side of the road while mom took off. We drove by slowly. The fawn was still, except for those huge brown eyes watching.

(Sunday, 9 A.M.) It is so still this A.M., it is eerie. We can hear water sounds to the west...runoff, most likely from Snow Camp Meadow.

Hiked to Snow Camp Meadow yesterday. Elk scat but no sightings. The meadow was carpeted with purple violets and yellow monkey-faced things. The cobra plants were past their prime but Bolander's lilies were nodding in the breeze. In our meandering, we must have seen seven different colors of Pacific iris, from deep purple through lavender, then lemony yellow and yellow diffused with purple, pure white and an amazing apricot color. A six inch salamander in the runoff stream has frilly purple gills. Rabbit, chipmunks and squirrels have been our only other companions. A few bird sounds...sparrowish. A lone turkey vulture braved the hard wind yesterday to see what was happening. Rufous also sighted towhee and a hummingbird.

June 12 - M. Family; Concord, CA

Watched cloud races. Beautiful ranges pockmarked by man's rape of old growth. Sorry to see all the cedar dying.

June 15 and 16 - Jean C. and Karen H.; Coos Bay, OR

(Jean) Too bad we didn't read the journals before hoofing it up the hill five trips with all our gear...we'd have known what to do with the wheelbarrow.

The evening light show made it all worthwhile, however. We came to photograph, each of us with about fifty extra pounds of cameras, tripods, lenses, filters, diffusers, etc., and we weren't disappointed. We "played with" an incredible rainbow for at least an hour and a half. From about 5:30 to 7 P.M. look 180 degrees from the sun in the vicinity of Red Mountain and Quail Prairie lookout; if there is mist or rain in the area, you're in luck. Our rainbow even had "God beams" running diagonally through it. Sure hope the photos do it justice!

We made it up for the sunrise, but "pooped out" by 7 A.M. and slept until 9 A.M. Quite refreshed, we headed off looking for the road to Snow Camp Meadow. No luck! But we did find Game Lake and although the sign warned of "narrow, rough road," we were pleasantly surprised to find it more than adequate for two wheel drive. We spent several hours photographing wild azaleas and rare white violets around the lake. On the drive out we stopped to photograph rhododendrons and were sidetracked by a colony of lovely windflowers. There are so many things to photograph and see.

This has been a wonderful visit and we found everything in good order. Thanks USFS and all the great visitors who left notes in the journal to read.

June 19, 20 and 21 - Susan, Dewinn, Glen (3), Graci (7), Melissa (10), Somessa (11) and Brooke (16); Brookings, OR

(Brooke) Well, we've had an interesting trip so far. First off, the gate was locked with a lock instead of a combination lock, so we had to drive all the way back to Gold Beach and call the Forest Service. Then drive all the way back up and wait for the key, but that wasn't too bad.

Next was the hill and unfortunately, we packed heavy. Even with the wheelbarrow from home, it wasn't much fun, but the cabin, view and everything else made up for everything.

This is my first time and it's been hard to pull my eyes away from the scenery for this long, so see you next time.

(Susan) I'm part of a group family of seven, two adults and five kids, who have had a great time here. We met "Timothy," had a perfectly clear day and one with clouds flowing over the mountains like marshmallows melting over hot chocolate. We saw boats on the ocean, had a great afternoon down at Hunter Creek and played cards till the lights didn't shine enough to see our hands. The walk up with the stuff for five kids was a bit much. Not till it was time to go did I wish even once they weren't all here with us.

There's propane fuel left over, clean towels we traded for some dubious ones and we're off for home.

110

June 21, 22 and 23 - Steven, DeEtta, Miranda (7) and Brian (6) W.; North Bend, OR

We found a small herd of elk crossing the road at Fairview Meadow. Got 'em all on the video-cam!

June 24 - Marc and Carolyn W.; North Bend, OR, and Peggy and Richard V.; Eugene, OR

We met "Timothy" this year (this is our third and our friend's fourth). Last year, we only heard him. This year he came out for some food in the evening. He also found a friend who is much more shy. We only heard this one in the wood and boxes at night. They helped themselves to some toilet paper and bits of a towel so they must be comfortable now...maybe babies are coming.

Anyway, it's Sunday now and we're about to leave. Back to the hustle and bustle.

The winds this morning were at 60 mph according to our gauge!

June 26 - Rick and Debbie R.; Harbor, OR

As we are here to celebrate Rick's fortieth birthday tomorrow, we were luckier than most...we left our teenagers home. As we drove off and left them, our fifteen year old son was going to call the cops and tell them we had abandoned them. We left anyway, smiling, cause we have not been away alone in over two years. I don't think the police would want our teenagers anyway. Ha! Ha!

It is nice being blessed with the sun and clear views. The flies are BIG!! Rick keeps getting up with the flyswatter and I keep ducking when he gets close in case he misses. At least by the time we leave tomorrow, Rick will be forty and I will be good at ducking. Everyone has to be good at something.

We had a good dinner...rum and Cokes and Hamm's beer. The peace and quiet up here are wonderful. Something we don't get much of around home! All we hear are the flies buzzing in the windows that Rick hasn't flattened yet. We are having a great time! Happy birthday to Rick...this was his birthday surprise from me. Just being alone with no children is a surprise itself.

Very relaxing place to be. We have a 4x4 Blazer so we didn't need kids to drive the wheelbarrow! Darn!

"Timothy" lives. Last night "Timothy" visited us!

We heard so much about the view from the potty that we had to take a picture from it.

We didn't hike anywhere. He who goes down the hill must come back up. Besides, the view is so pretty, who wants to leave.

June 27 and 28 - Jeff and Theresa S.; Crescent City, CA

We've been married exactly two days and I'm already playing pack horse. But I guess that's what I get for being half an hour late to my own wedding.

The hike up was well worth it as you can see. Mother earth has truly blessed us. It's very, very sad to see how man has stripped her. Aside from the clearcuts, this is the most beautiful place for a honeymoon. I could stay forever.

By the way, we had quite a noisy dinner guest last night, must have been "Timothy." Anyhow, he didn't stay long or eat much; so as far as dinner guests go, "Timothy" is OK.

Also, this is a great place to burn the buns.

June 29 - S. and M.; Durham, NC

Earning a bath. So the Ford Explorers of nowadays have marginal equipment, i.e., the stones on our adventure to bathe waxed our two right side tires. Changed one and limped to Gold Beach. We had one psi of air in the right rear tire on arrival to the Exxon oasis. Funny that, because the guy there fixed the two flats in forty minutes and asked for $10. This from that pariah of a corporation. You just never know.

By the way, we got the payoff immersion in Hunter's Creek. A most joyous dip. I once again give thanks for the great goodness that surrounds us, even though at times in this "stewardship of the land" I see great wounding and a struggle to recover.

July 2, 3 and 4 - Rod and Linda; Salem, OR

Someone else canceled their reservation and we were able to spend a three day weekend at this wonderful spot.

We found a mouse nest in the drawer beneath the table...I dumped it. Hope no one minds, but "Timothy" (or his wife), can live outside!

We didn't hike anywhere...we knew it'd be hot down from this mountaintop. We were lazy and read, napped, played cards and ate...just what we needed. Like most, our lives are too busy and this was one terrific stress-reducing getaway!!

July 4 and 5 - Peter, Teresa and Kia; Kelso, WA

Well, we've returned again and actually got reservations on July 4th like we'd planned last year.

"Timothy" was here. Next year we'll remember the roll of screen I

112

wanted to bring this year and a glue trap for dear ol' "Timothy."

We stayed at Elko Camp the night before Snow Camp. There is a crystal clear drinking water spring directly across from the Elko Camp sign.

It has been clear and windy, up to 60 mph, both days. The new wind gauge is a bonus since last year. We watched the fireworks from Crescent City and Brookings. Not much sign of wildlife this trip unless you count the giant killer horseflies which are big enough to take care of themselves.

See our previous entry for June 23, 1993.

July 6 - Meriwether F.; Portland, OR

Hi! My name is Meriwether F. and I'm ten years old. I'm in fourth grade or I guess I should say, I was in fourth grade.

It took my mom, my brother and I a whole six hours to get here. It was boring.

We finally arrived here at 5 P.M. What a ride!

That night, the wind was scaring my brother and I. It seemed like the wind speed was going 50 mph but it was going the same speed it did when we got here.

I'm a young author. I write poems and stories.

—A New Baby—

Dad get's a baby. Mom get's off work. I got to stay home and be treated like dirt. I sit in a corner, while mom has a shower. Dad get's to throw her for hours and hours. Uncle Sam came in and then Uncle Finster and I, I got a kiss from my new baby sister.

July 7, 8, 9 and 10 - Torrie and Bob; Salem, OR

We came, we saw, we did it all! (For this year anyway.) We watched sunsets, sunrises, the Milky Way cross the sky. We saw squirrels, chipmunks, a deer in the parking area and "Timothy" (or his cousin) on the deck during a night jaunt to the outhouse. Vultures scouted us out (we told the little dog to keep moving), and a couple of mama quail vied for the Academy Award for best portrayal of an injured bird.

We hiked to Snow Camp Meadow and out the other side; down to Windy Valley from Mineral Mountain and while we explored that meadow, mother nature steepened the return trail! We sought Panther Lake (is it now a meadow?), and did find Game Lake.

We napped and read and ate. We smelled the azaleas and cedars. We listened to the wind shake, rattle and roll our home...60 mph gusts last night.

Last year we had one night here...this year three. Don't know if we'll be back but we sure have great memories!

July 11, 12 and 13 - Greg, Jesse, Jami and Lloyd; Myrtle Creek, OR

Jesse is nine years old...wants to live here forever. Can't say I disagree. The dogs (3) have also enjoyed their stay. They always go camping with us. Jami, he's 17, is having a tough time in the morning wind...just about pushed him over the west side. Wish we didn't have to leave today.

July 13 - Paul (64) and Anita (54) S.; Salinas, CA, and Scott (27) with "Biscuit," the Black Lab; Wilderville, OR

(July 13, 10 P.M.) Arrived at 1 P.M. and the adventures started immediately. As dad (Paul) pushed a load of gear up the hill in the wheelbarrow, he stopped to move a rock that was in his path. A combination of the wind and gravity proceeded to tip the wheelbarrow over backwards, sending a parade of sleeping bags, dishes and food down the hill. The lone casualty was the Tupperware bowl full of chili that was supposed to be our dinner. We got to the bowl before all the chili poured out, salvaged about half of it and still ate well come supper time. Still, I think we were all glad we decided for a lunch stop at the Brookings McDonald's before we headed up here.

After we unloaded the Subaru, eliminated the biting horseflies and enjoyed our first glimpses of the incredible panorama, we set out for Fairview Meadow. The Enchanted Forest was very serene. Then it was onto the Darlingtonia bog, where we saw literally dozens of these rare plants. It was an extremely satisfying afternoon.

As the evening progresses, the wind is hammering the lookout with steadily increasing ferocity. For the past two hours, the structure has been shaking in sustained winds of 50 to 55 mph and numerous gusts of 67 and 68 mph. The wind gauge has mom fascinated. As I use the flashlight to write this, she is lighting matches so she can see the gauge, hoping for the so-far-elusive 70 mph gust. Finally, no sign of "Timothy"...yet.

(July 14 - 9 A.M.) The wind has been relentless. Sustained speed of 50 mph and this morning, mom saw the gauge hit 72 mph during one gust. It makes a trip to the bathroom a full out adventure.

July 15 and 16 - Markus B. and Lore; Switzerland and Grants Pass, OR

Shasta, our five year old retriever/shepherd, does not like curves and so she whined and panted the entire trip over the Galice-Agness road and then the lookout road. Opi, the puppy (mutt), was quiet...turns out she's a silent sufferer and about seven miles shy of Snow Camp she got sick in the car. After cleanup, we're back on our way and made it about 8:45 P.M. *Very* glad to get here.

Forty to forty-five mph winds greet us. We get unpacked, make some coffee and settle in for a discussion of when the wind should stop. It didn't.

Sunset was quick, but nice. Up at 5 A.M. with the first light. Sunrise was nice too. Back to sleep after a waffle/fruit salad breakfast, lazing around reading magazines and books. Around 11 A.M. we go exploring…get some relief from the wind. Over at Game Lake the dogs go swimming and "play stick." We hike around a bit. Return to camp at 3 P.M. and voilà! No wind! Instead there are many flies. We have to open the windows and doors because it's very hot. We'll get used to the flies. Around 6 P.M., the wind's back up to 20 mph and by 7 P.M. it's at 40 mph again. Presto! No flies.

No sign of "Timothy" but we do see ants, maybe carpenter ants, taking out chunks of the window pane on the west side.

Markus decides to sleep on the west side balcony for part of the night. It's cooler out there. Up again at first light, back to sleep after sunrise.

Best view and quietest neighbors of any motel we've ever been to.

Next destination, Pearsoll Peak, in three weeks. Can't imagine it can match this.

Author's note: Pearsoll Peak's lookout restoration was finished and made available to the public on August 6, 1994. Markus and Lore made the first entry in that journal. You can see Pearsoll Peak from Snow Camp by looking east southeast across the Kalmiopsis Wilderness. You can make out the lookout with a telescope or a good pair of binoculars. It sits right on the eastern edge of the Kalmiopsis Wilderness and requires a greater effort to spend a night there.

*One route is from Selma (on the Redwood Highway which runs from Grants Pass, OR to Crescent City, CA), down the Illinois River. Once you cross the river, you need a 4x4 vehicle and be prepared for hours of snail-pace driving to go a mere six miles — **very** rugged. When you arrive in the "parking area," you have approximately another mile of uphill hiking to get to the lookout. The view again is spectacular and the serpentine soils in the area are extremely interesting in themselves. It is available June 1 to November 1. After October 1, a road closure is in effect due to Port Orford cedar disease, so access is by hiking from Onion Camp only.*

For additional information, contact the Illinois Valley Ranger District, 26568 Redwood Hwy., Cave Junction, OR 97523; phone (541) 592-2166.

I stayed there two nights, from September 20 to 22, and found it an excellent place to work on this book. I had total privacy and the telephone never rang once.

July 19 and 20 - Doug and Kathi; Los Angeles, CA, and Ginny and Dottie; McHenry, IL

Well, we finally arrived after beating all the odds. First, we misunderstood our directions, misread our map and went towards Grants Pass from Crescent City instead of Brookings. Next, our van, which was pulling a seventeen foot camper, overheated continuously on the road, causing us to abandon the camper on the way up. Next, a flat tire on the van which needed a special tool to change it...which we did not have. (Chrysler!!) So, in our other vehicle (Honda), we drove back to Brookings and paid $300 for a tow down the mountain and a new tire. At that point, we still had a great deal of enthusiasm which quickly subsided into tears and stress-induced bickering as the van began to heat up again about nine miles south of Snow Camp — even lacking the trailer!!

We spent two nights in the Prairie Creek while all these shenanigans were occurring. Today, on the third day of our three day rental, we decided to forego the vehicles and hike up here from the 1103 Snow Camp lookout trail. The map said "five miles—difficult" and they weren't kidding. We finally arrived, after a four hour hike — all continually uphill (1,000 feet); we were overheating as much as our vehicles in the 100 degree heat. As we saw Snow Camp from a half mile away, we really didn't know if we would make it. *But we did* and damn it, we really earned this splendid view.

This is truly the most peace-inspiring place I've ever experienced. After planning to spend three nights here and only getting to spend one, I am torn between feeling cheated and being grateful for at least one night here.

July 26 - Jean and Larry; Eugene, OR

It's our third visit to Snow Camp, planned this time around the full moon which has risen as an orange ball of fire and shown brightly each night.

Drove to Brookings, stopped at Quail Prairie Lookout on return trip. Visited a few minutes with the friendly folks doing fire watch. This area has quite an interesting history!

Hiked to Windy Valley...on a hot, sunny day, it felt like thirteen miles instead of three each way. Two plus quarts of water was not enough.

Sunsets and sunrises...brilliant orange strips on the horizons. Moon sets as sun rises.

Some very helpful luxuries...we put screen on windows with duct tape and solar showers, which felt great. Our jazz tapes and great wine contributed to the evening's enjoyment as well.

116

July 29 - Wally and Jeanne; Coburg, OR

Having grown up in a lookout family, it is a real treat to be on a lookout again. When I retire I want my old job back!

And without the wind, it would be miserable and often flying ants would invade. So praise the wind!

Mopped the floor on our way out and left next folks some water.

August 8 - Cary and Shelly; Applegate, OR

(Cary) We made it here without any flat tires or lock problems and it has been paradise. I love the room with a view! Yesterday we hiked in Fairview Meadows and were entranced following elk prints but didn't see any elk. Then we adventured over to the Enchanted Forest where there was a parked car with someone in it. We were apprehensive (being from cities) about approaching the car which was in our pathway, but we decided to go for it. A blond haired woman stepped out of the car; she was alone and asked us if we had seen a plaque on any of the trees in the meadow. She looked sad and somewhat distraught. We hadn't seen any plaque and told her so. She then looked even more sad. We wanted to ask her more about it, but really didn't know what to ask!

We ventured on through the Enchanted Forest, weaving through trees and admiring all of the beauty. On our way back, Shelly saw the plaque — it's about twenty feet high — in a tree. It's a beautiful plaque…gold and green. The way the sun was hitting it though, it was difficult to read and you definitely needed binoculars to read it. All I was able to decipher was that it was there in loving memory of someone named Lawson. There is a lot more writing and we are going back this morning hoping for better light to read the rest.

When you reach the Enchanted Forest, there is a roadway going into what looks like an old campground area. Once you're in the tree area, look for one of the biggest trees, straight ahead; walk behind that tree, look up and you'll see the plaque. If anyone has more information about this person or plaque, it would be interesting to log it. We only hope that the woman was able to find it to put her heart at ease, for she was gone by the time we returned and found it.

Next was Snow Camp Meadow. Wow! Spectacular! The plants were outrageous and the view of the lookout from down in the meadow is worth seeing; all in all, we hiked, played and explored with great love and appreciation for all.

Thank you Mother Earth, Father Sky, the beautiful stars, sunrise, sunset and the peacefulness. Also, thank you David and Barbara for this gift. It's one that will always be remembered.

Oh, and a note to "Timothy…." Watch out!! By the north window…it's a trap!!!

(Shelly) The moment I got here I knew I didn't want to go home tomorrow. I thought about becoming a national headline "Lady won't leave lookout…two dead, update at 11 P.M." But back to reality, ya know…did O.J. do it?

> As for the sunset
> What a surprise
> As the sun tipped his hat
> And the wink with his eyes
> He spoke with a whisper
> See ya both at sunrise.

P.S. About the outhouse, the floor is funky and that's OK…but the seat was never put in the right place (see middle).

Authors note: The seat in the outhouse is to the left so you find yourself leaning to the right to capture the full essence of the view (with the door open, of course).

August 9 - Dennis, Gabe and Elijah A.; Applegate, OR

(Dennis) Only time for a quick entry, indicative of how the trip has gone…too quick, too fast…but we loved it! Another nice experience on the mountain. Thanks again David and Barbara for thinking of us and making this all possible.

Brought our guitars and filled these glass walls with live music most the night. Some oldies, some goodies and a little bit of punk, which kind of describes the occupants.

(Gabe) Off to Eugene to see Chaos U.K. tonight.

August 10, 11, 12 and 13 - "Rangers" David and Barbara; Applegate and Grants Pass, OR

(David) Hello Snow Camp, we are back (see September 23 and 24, 1993). We've been looking forward all year to this time together up here. And yes, for anyone who read our 1993 entries, we are even **more** in love with each other. Oh, Barbara, how I love thee….

Yesterday we had two large groups of visitors around midday. They came to admire the view, didn't stay long, thank you.

We took the truck to Fairview Meadow yesterday. Found the plaque on the tree that Shelly and Cary (our friends) spoke about. It says:

118

Lane Whitney Lawson
Son of Roy and Joy Lawson
Born June 24, 1967 in Johnson City, Tenn.
Died May 29, 1994 At This Spot
Fairview Meadow Camp
Leaving Behind His Loving
Friends and Fellow Practitioners
Of the Northern Tai Chi Tum Pai Gung
May This Camp Area Forever Be Blessed
And Hold His Good Spirit

I do hope the lady found the plaque and peace.

Shortly after we left Fairview Meadow, we came upon a herd of fifteen to twenty elk cows and calves. Perhaps Lane's spirit ran with them.

Thank you Mother Nature/Earth for our time here. (More later, two days to go.)

Must leave tomorrow, don't want to go. Life is so "rat racy" down there. Been watching for "falling stars" each night. Saw thirty-three last night and twenty-six the night before in about one hour's time both nights. WOW!

Today we left for the afternoon. When we came back, we had been locked out at the gate with the Forest Service padlock (the combination lock had been put back in such a way as to render it useless.) Suspect the driver of the "potty wagon." Imagine the frustration of coming back late, and finding yourself locked out, your equipment locked in. I managed to break the FS lock with my PTO winch, whew! Have read two other entries with "locked out" experiences. Need to take "their locks" away from them and have them use a combination like the rest of us??

The days have been perfect. Always clear up here. Usually foggy down below but it burns off by midday. Lots of smoke over toward Cave Junction and the Rogue Valley area. Here's praying we get through this summer with no more forest fires.

Did you notice, there are 111 panes of glass to wash in this building, times two (in and out).

Can see eleven boats out on the ocean tonight, beyond the fog. Don't think I'd care to be on one if the sea was rough at all. Takes all kinds.

Tired. Didn't do much today but I'll sleep very well. Must be this wonderful mountain.

(Barbara) Saturday morning has come too quickly. Our stay, spanning five, warm, windless, blue skied days, is coming to an end. Like all who have had this experience here, we don't want to leave and like last time, a part of us won't. The best part is sharing all this beauty, peace and nature with my lover, David. We've sure had fun, laughed and enjoyed each other's company. A little part, actually a big part for me, of this trip was to catch the meteor showers. All in all, I had the pleasure of seeing some 150 "falling stars." There were yellow ones, blue tailed ones, little short ones, long glowing ones and some so bright they left a ghost image for seconds afterward against the black night sky. And we did it in style, I must say. Lounge chairs, sleeping bags zipped together for warmth of course, and oh, can't forget the stocking "snow" caps. Just like being kids again some _____ years ago! What a wonderful gift we have...all this beauty...just a little motivation and **recall.**

We missed our little buddy, "Timothy" this year. Perhaps he and the little family are in the meadows on vacation.

There is so much I could write about, but will keep this short as there is packing up to do, a lunch to make and most important, some rays to be caught.

Thank you, David, for bringing me here, I do love you so...hope to be back next year. To all the children, thank you for your entries in the journal, and especially your art work! Isn't this place awesome?

P.S. And Vinnie, David's DOG, was a great addition this year. Maybe I could be a dog person after all.

August 13 - Sonia, Jana, Tara and John; Eugene, OR

We spotted it as we were about a third of the way up from the Jeep bringing up the first load of gear. We noticed the dark layered smoke on the eastern horizon as we drove in. But now, there was the source. It was putting up layered smoke between five and six thousand feet. In just the few minutes it took to reach the lookout, a small but ugly brown column began to build above the layered smoke. We turned the firefinder and sighted the smoke at 146 degrees. It was coming up from behind the farthest horizon and off of the maps we had available; I placed the range at about sixty miles out...California.

In just the few minutes it takes to turn the azimuth, the column that had just begun to appear, now stands dominant above the layered smoke of before. Two times the height of the layered smoke, it continues to grow. It peaks out at a vertical angle of $+4\frac{1}{2}$ degrees with white cap for all the world to see.

Somewhere, there to the southeast, in California, a large forest fire is taking a major run. For those souls who toil there on those thirsty slopes...get out of its way! For when nature has the bit in her teeth, there is

120

nothing that you can do. Get out of the way and wait and look for another opportunity!

After arriving and spotting the fire in California, our time was busy here. Busy as a twenty month old and a four year old about to turn five, can make it. As we prepare to leave, we are happy to report that we had beautiful weather both day and night.

It should also be recorded here that these glass walls reverberated with squeals and laughter of our little girls and that the sounds of little feet running around and around the catwalk have echoed down these mountain slopes. And just there, in front of the double doors of the low cabinet, my little Tara stood in the early morning sun waving at her shadow on the cabinet as it waved back to her.

Good-bye Snow Camp! Thanks!

August 16 - Christine H. and Steve K.; Chatsworth, CA

Wow! After all these journal entries (yes, I read them all), I could just say "DITTO"…but I won't. We arrived Monday, August 15, around 10 P.M., after fixing a flat on the way up that dirt road (oh well, I guess I needed to get a new one sometime).

It's 9:30 P.M. now as I sip my chardonnay and wait for a feast of chili dogs. Maybe not a gourmet style dinner but we never thought this lookout would be so well equipped and homey. What a refreshing surprise! This is our first trip to the "room with a view" but definitely not our last! I can't decide if I want to tell everyone I meet about this enchanted "hideaway" or simply be selfish and save it for the truly appreciative.

Mouse ↓

Where are the paper products?

Tomorrow Steve and I will rise early…whether we like it or not (we do/we don't). We'll savor a little Wheaties with some fresh peaches and a one-of-kind sunrise. We plan to hike to Snow Camp Meadow and hopefully discover the Enchanted Forest.

Although we got a flat (as did many others), we got to gander at five cows (who were gandering back), and four deer (so grateful), on the road up. Yea, there was a few horseflies trying to pick a fight but I let them know who's boss as I unsuccessfully swatted my sweatshirt at them and ran for my life.

How did everyone find out about this amazing place? We found an article in the travel section of the *Daily News* in the San Fernando Valley.

Although we be from Californy, we too can enjoy the scenery. We drove two days to get here. Even spent a night at the Union Square Hotel in San Francisco (nice place), but nothing compares to Hotel Snow Camp! We were prepared for a drafty wooden shack (and would have been quite content), so arriving here to tiled floors, furniture (a bed to kill for on any camping trip), and 360 degrees of window space is icing on the cake.

"How now, Brown Cow?"

Beware of the wild Siskiyou mountain Cow!

Swish

I wish we had more than just a bottle of beer to contribute! It is truly a privilege to be allowed to stay here. The drive from L.A. was worth it. Don't worry, nobody I know would make that drive to go *camping*. Oregon is safe...*for now*.

"♨ Bzzz"

"Amana, git! You! (Sucka)"

We played Yahtzee, drank, ate, talked, biked, hiked, read, stared, thought, sought, fought...made up. We took a ba-jillion pictures, looked through our binoculars and sat in silence just listening to the wind and the occasional bird "fighting" the wind. One thing...BIG WIND, no mosquitoes! We loved it!

Thank you Snow Camp! I will treasure the memories of such complete serenity. Thank you Wayne Spencer, fire staff lookout, 1980 to 1990 (see plaque on firefinder), for his persistence, and thank all the previous renters for their generous donations. May Snow Camp be here for my children to one day enjoy.

August 19 - Susan and Scott; Gresham, OR

We arrived last night around 7 P.M. with beautiful skies. The moon was nearly full, illuminating our view all evening until dawn when the clouds rolled in along with 30 mph winds. (It was fun seeing clouds *shooting* past our windows.) What a place!

I must say, I stressed driving our two seater Pontiac Fiero (maybe six inch clearance underneath)! After reading most of this journal and by the time I came to the fourth group who'd experienced a flat tire, I felt really grateful (later, up to eight flats...worst was July 19, 1994, what a bummer...). Just as a curiosity, I did walk down the hill and checked the tires this morning...all inflated.

Thanks to our friend, Jill, for sending us the newspaper clipping several years back; really glad we finally made it. I will also state as many others have in this fun-to-read journal...it's nice to be away from telephones!!!! I also am happy to leave behind the TV. It somehow seems socially acceptable however, to bring a small piece of civilization in the form of a radio. We too experienced fantastic radio reception with stations as far away as Idaho, Washington, California and Kalispell, Montana. Scott suggested an old CB radio may someday be donated to Snow Camp for guests to listen to if desired. (Could also be used to call for fires or serious physical injuries).

Scott chopped some wood for exercise, enough to probably last two days.

Earlier this month, a guest wrote of a trap for "Timothy," the famous camp critter. This was a sad thing to read. Was "Timothy" in our home or were we in "Timothy's?"

We hope more of these lookouts can be utilized for the pleasure of all who appreciate beauty and quiet.

August 20 - Les, Kay, Charlie and Gaia G. (also starring Comet, the Wonder Dog); Medford, OR

We arrived out-of-breath because we didn't realize we could open the gate! The second trip to the car, I took a closer look at the lock... same combination as the door! Then we arrived the second time out-of-breath because we were hauling too much of our "bare necessities." By the time we shoved all our gear in the door, the sun decided to reward our efforts with a beautiful setting. Aaahh...it was worth it for that alone.

Thanks to Kathleen D. for turning us onto this incredible aesthetic adventure. I found out about it at the last minute, before embarking on a more mundanely planned trip to the coast. For a family of non-risk-taking comfort lovers like us, this was truly a "new leaf turning." By the way, there is a perfect full moon gazing balefully in the window at me as I write this.

My wife, Kay, is impressed by the cotton batting shawls that adorn the shoulders of the surrounding mountains. I can't wait to read the comments of our predecessors in the morning when I won't need to hold this silly flashlight to see.

Gaia spoke to us today.

August 28, 29, 30 and 31 - Matthew, Aida, Julio, Mike and Elwood R-H.; Eureka, CA

(August 31 - 10:05 A.M.) The wind has performed its morning alchemy again, going from a steady 30-40 mph at 8:30 A.M. to 5-10 mph now.

Wind— has been the defining element of our stay here, though the other elements have also been actively represented.

Fire— Our first evening's dinner preparations were redirected when we discovered a pinhole leak in the tank of the Coleman three-burner stove we borrowed from our friends. However, the combination of fir firewood and the wood stove here soon rectified that. We ended up having a breakfast fire and a dinner fire each night, usually leaving the windows and door open to prevent sauna conditions.

Water— Traveling with two boys, ages 6½ and 8½, one an avid fisherman, the other an avid wanna-be, meant that water and its pleasures played a major role in our itinerary. Swimming in the Chetco on the way up at Little Redwood, then heading down to the Chetco Gorge trail head Monday, to do catch and release with salamanders, snakes, freshwater lobsters, etc. Good swimming spot for the adults as well. Then yesterday, Tuesday, we headed for Game Lake, for more water fun for kids, trail fun for adults, until the other element came into play.

Earth— In the form of rocks. The sharp edges of the serpentine roadbed took their toll on one of our tires about three to four miles from the lake — consternation, palaver, mounting of the pseudo-spare. Eventually, responsibility reigned and we decided to drive to Gold Beach and get it patched. Julio and Elwood didn't mind when we told them our lake picnic would turn into an ocean picnic. Down the seemingly interminable Hunter Creek Road, through the land of cutblocks (clearcuts?), and eventually to Gold Beach, where the Exxon (in the process of turning into Shell), station fixed us up. Then on to the ocean, where the wind was blowing even stronger than up here, 40 to 50 mph gusts. Found a spot in the lee of the rocks, kids frolicked, adults pondered the fluid reality and drank beer. Then back to the mountain for another lovely sunset, another lovely dinner and another lovely sleep.

And now it's 10:30. Checkout time approaches. Our son just came up to tell us we have another flat. Tee hee!

Anything I add about the lookout and its charms would just reprise the words of earlier writers. The journal is a joy, as is the lookout and the qualities of stewardship it brings out in its sojourners.

We will return. Yes, we will return...with thick tires!

August 31 and September 1 - Tracy and Morgan R.; Brookings, OR

I and my son, Morgan, are here for the second time this year. Today we hiked to Snow Camp Meadow with our geriatric dog, nice and slow and carrying him part of the way...he ain't heavy, he's my puppy.

September 4, 5 and 6 - Monty, Judi, Bud and Edie P.; Coos Bay, OR

(Edie) We arrived at 12 noon on the fourth...worked hard to get gate open. Wrong directions for combination lock, but we don't give up easily.

Bud is an eighty-year old Curry County native. He came up the hill with a backpack as easily as any young person could. Edie is a seventy-seven year old and surprisingly was able to come up the hill with a pack (nowhere near as heavy as Bud's).

We are here to celebrate our fifty-sixth anniversary, thanks to our daughter-in-law, Judi, and Monty. They are both fifty-year olds and celebrating their thirty-first anniversary, although it is a few months late.

After two trips up the hill with heavy loads, Judi and I stayed up. Bud and Monty each packed up four loads. (Do we need all this stuff?)

The sunset was fabulous and lasted so long with all the beautiful shades of pinks, blues, lavenders and every shade of red by the time it sank into the ocean.

(Monty) I've been called off center, crazy, having a warped sense of humor and any number of other wonderful terms, but I think it takes a little of all of these to appreciate the view from the top. We've hunted in these hills for over thirty years, viewing this lookout from every angle...but this angle is the best.

We've read the entries about "Timothy" but haven't seen him. I believe "Timothy's" Leary.

I've also read entries about trees, wind, elk and the view from the outhouse. All I can say in closing is while sitting there looking through the door, I just may be slightly off center.

(Judi) What an experience! Somebody "up there" must really love us to have provided such a perfect setting for a wonderful weekend!

I saw where other campers had left food and other supplies...I can sure see why. I'm all for leaving all we brought although the trip down is a lot easier. Last night I wheeled the "barrow" up with pop and water. I thought it was to be my "last" act on this earth but what a beautiful place to die! Next year I'm coming as a much fitter, thinner, nonsmoker and I'm not going to pack more than we need!

Bud would like to stay up here for a couple of months in the winter and watch it snow.

September 22 - Bob M.; Grants Pass, OR

I came alone to think, ponder, etc. I'll be back too, but doubt I'll ever get Joyce up here...too high and windy for her! Wouldn't want to bring the kids.

September 23 - Beverly B.; Eugene, OR

I came up here for many reasons: to read in peace in a place wherever, whenever I glance up from my books, my eyes are filled with wonder; to have an excuse not to speak for three days; to breathe air *this* clean; to be in a room full of windows; to listen to wind sing; to await the red, red moon in the east; to walk around in my underwear for as long as I like; to write and write and write without interruption; to eat the food I like as the sun goes down; to watch the weather pass, the fog fill the valleys and retreat again; to have this good a view from the toilet; to do absolutely *nothing*; to get as close to nirvana as a human can; to rest before I begin to teach again in the fall; to finally release the husband and the home I left in July; to mark the gateway between the life I used to live and the life I have yet to live; to get a tan; to eat alone by candlelight; to breathe in and breathe out, assuming the pattern of tides; to type on my "Royal" above 4000 feet; to practice chopping wood without losing a toe (yet); to marvel at all the constellations I don't know; to bathe in two gallons of drinking water; to read the stories of those who have come before; to snooze in my sleeping bag with the duck print flannel lining; to eat chips and salsa for breakfast; *to begin my life anew.*

September 28 - Graig and Barbara D.; Cave Junction, OR

It is always an adventure to come to Snow Camp. Two years ago, at this time of year, we came up here and enjoyed a beautiful sunset. Then came the headlights of a vehicle, all the way up to the door. It was a state police officer who wanted to use the lookout to check for poachers. Finally he left. When we arrived on Monday, two days ago, to spend a two night adventure, we found **another** couple already here. Surprise! The Forest Service apparently double-booked the lookout. They had a signed permit in hand that said they had the lookout for the night. We had our signed permit that said we had the lookout for the night. They were hardly gracious about the circumstances. Rather, they made it seem like it was our fault. They had the advantage though, as they had already moved into the lookout. We camped in the parking lot.

OK, we're going to have a chat with the FS folks when this is over. At least we have one night in the lookout.

Spent yesterday exploring the area. Had a great lunch at Game Lake, then went down to the Rogue River. Went to Gold Beach, then came back up Hunter's Creek Road. Driving back to the lookout, we grew worried thinking someone else may be in the lookout. Luckily, no, so we moved in and began cooking dinner with the threat of a storm approaching off the ocean.

Went to sleep about 10 P.M. Awoke with a start at 2 A.M. to the crash of thunder. What a light show. Scary too! Stayed in bed and watched the lightning strike all the surrounding mountains. Prayed it would miss this one. The storm continued for more than four hours, with the last of the flashes ending after sunrise. Finally, I've enough courage to head for the head.

Ah! Silence. Time to be alone…not quite. About 8:30 A.M. a FS law enforcement officer, Ray, came by to check for "smokes," which would indicate where fires were set by lightning.

It is now 11 A.M. We've had breakfast under Ray's watchful eye. Now he's sitting in his rig, just a few feet from the picnic table, motor running to charge his battery.

Got to finish packing and get out of here. The fog is rolling in thick. Maybe we'll do this again. We'd love to experience the solitude.

September 29, 30, October 1 and 2 - Wayne and Carol; Medford, OR

Third year here and it's still beautiful although I'm not sure it's the place to come to be alone! We arrived here Thursday at 1 P.M. It was raining real hard and the lookout was really socked in. Thursday from 1 P.M. to 6 P.M. we were visited by five different people. Two Forest Service men were at the gate when we came. We chatted in the rain, met one person who was coming downhill after working on the building. About 3 P.M., two men came up to work on the equipment. They apologized for the intrusion. The clouds cleared off and it was a beautiful star filled night.

(Friday) Woke up to a beautiful day, ate breakfast. Wayne went for a walk to find Panther Lake. Two men came up at noon to flush out the outhouse, stayed a half hour and talked for a while. A state forester from Medford came up at 4:45 P.M. to work on the equipment in the building, had no key; they had changed the locks, and was here a half hour. He then drove down to meet someone bringing the key. He came back and was here till 8:15 P.M. repairing equipment. He even climbed up the tower in the dark with winds at 40 mph to fix the antenna.

(Saturday) Nobody has come to visit yet today. The reason for all the visitors, except for the toilet men, is because the lightning on Wednesday night struck the antenna on the communications building and damaged the antenna and the equipment inside. Sort of glad I wasn't here for that show. Apparently no one was here Wednesday night.

Gonna work on a puzzle now, did the dishes, made the bed, even swept and mopped. Must be going crazy.

(Saturday - 2:45 P.M.) Well, shit! I'm puzzling. My hubby is in his underwear laying on the bed reading and what do we hear? "Hey, how far is it to Gold Beach?" Guess what…man, woman and dog walked up right to the door which was open. I don't believe it. Where do you have to go for privacy? Need to hang a sign on the gate "Lookout occupied, please do not disturb!" We did last year. We can understand the ones that need to do a job. Although the amount of people, five Thursday, four Friday, two today, is a bit overwhelming.

(Wayne - October 2) What a crummy place, no billboards anywhere. No noise, except for the wind gusting to 55 mph, and dangerous! Lightning struck not only this mountain but the antenna outside as well. People from the Quail Prairie Lookout said they were watching great blue balls of lightning striking all over this ridge. The thunder was so loud it sounded like it was coming from inside your head. A shattering psychological experience reducing brave men to whimpers. There is something wrong with the air here too…too much oxygen I think.

We would have had more privacy at the Rogue Valley Shopping Mall. Assholes walk up to the door and begin conversation like we are dying to make their acquaintance. Why we came all this way and locked a gate behind us to meet and greet strangers! Unfathomable. Of course, these people feel righteously indignant when you are less than gracious. "Tell me your life story," they want you to say. "I'll bet you are a very interesting person that I would be greatly enriched by knowing…right?"

I want my MTV! I wonder what news I've missed that will make me more ignorant?

There sure is a lot of dirt up here. Especially on the ground. Weird.

This was penned by Wayne the Pain, Healer of the Halt and the Lame.

October 3 - Jody P.; Grants Pass, OR

Here I am, a grown woman sitting up at 10:30 P.M., (while husband snores away), reading this journal, trying to find some comfort. I'm saying Catholic prayers and still scared to death. It feels like I'm riding in a glass freight train in the sky!!! I'm dead tired from lugging everything up and down that hill but I don't know how I'm gonna sleep tonight…wish I'd brought some brandy. The wind is gusting to 65 on the wind indicator and it sounds like Halloween with someone constantly trying to get in the front door. No moon, so it's very dark but the stars are staying in place.

In fact, this place is haunted. It's turned husband and I into a couple of entranced ghosts floating from window to window, not bothering to sit…afraid we might miss something.

We had a big shaggy bear run in front of the car for awhile and narrowly avoided Bambi and his mom, which got our springer spaniel puppy very excited.

It's neat to watch the occasional bird fly in this wind. Puppy and I walked to the meadow/valley junction and would've liked to have gotten an earlier start...maybe next spring when there will be wildflowers. There were wonderful little chickadees all around us. I found some berries, dark purple-red, bell shaped, sweet and tart, leaf like, slightly thick. What are they? I'm not sick yet. I wish there was a book of native plants kept here.

We came for solitude, quiet and peace. God! Will this wind never cease? Of course logic took over (or perhaps the prayers worked) and I finally got to sleep. The wind dies down right when we are leaving.

(Husband)

Twisted manzanita and furs a few,
Down below, the world's askew,
But here there's tranquillity at last,
Hopes for my future have been cast.
I shall stay forever in my dreams,
On Snow Camp Mountain and scenes.

and

Seated one morning on the john,
The view and I exploded and went on,
With the door open and view serene,
The happiest time that's ever been.

October 6 and 7 - Linda and Glenn T.; Gold Beach, OR

Interestingly enough, before I ever read this journal, my husband's first order of business was to raise "Old Glory" to its rightful place. And so we close out Snow Camp's 1994 season with the same heartfelt reason the first camper of this season did (June 2, 3 and 4, 1994).

We saw a hawk hovering for the longest time over a valley below us...really neat to see! Amazing capabilities that various beings on earth have, ya know?

This is our twenty-seventh wedding anniversary today. I'm totally charmed by this whole experience of ours! Thank you, thank you, rangers and previous occupants who have stocked this lookout with all the amenities that you did! Lovely...lovely sojourn!

October 9 - Lisa, Lena, Bill, Anna and John; North Bend, OR

(John) This is the best spot in the world to listen to Zeppelin's *Misty Mountain Hop!*

October 18 - David Calahan (author of this book); Applegate, OR

Dear Snow Camp. So nice to visit you again this year. As usual, your weather was perfect for me. I'd like to have a lightning show next time. I'm told I'm either the last or next to the last paying guest this year. The weather was so nice, the Forest Service extended the normal closing time, which is usually the first of October. Since I was here last on August 13, 1994, you have not changed much. So nice to see all the amenities still here, plus a few more added.

This place has a special meaning for me and I suspect it will become even more so. I wish Barbara could have come with me. Being alone this trip has its own unique feeling, but I miss her.

Many thanks go to the Forest Service, volunteers and cooperative guests for keeping Snow Camp alive and healthy.

That was the last entry for Snow Camp's 1994 season.

GENERAL HISTORY
OF THE SNOW CAMP AREA

The archeological record attests to a continuous human occupation of southwest Oregon for the past 9000 years. The oldest dates of
occupation have been unearthed at the Marial site, approximately
twenty-five miles northeast of Snow Camp. Research in the Pistol
River drainage at the Curtday Acorn Site, approximately five and one-
half miles to the west, indicates occupation for at least 4000 years.

Prehistorically, the area around Snow Camp was occupied by
Athapaskan and Penutian speaking bands of the Tututni. The Tututni
occupied a large area of southwest Oregon utilizing the coastal areas
from south of present day Bandon to northern California and extending inland following the major rivers such as the Rogue, Illinois,
Chetco and Pistol. These were separate bands of people speaking
different dialects of the Athapaskan language.

The general pattern of Tututni settlement indicates that large,
permanent winter villages were established along coastal areas, rivers
and major streams. Seasonally, inhabitants would leave the lowland
villages for upland areas to gather a variety of plant foods and other
plant products, as well as raw materials for the production of stone
tools. Big game hunting was also an upland occupation.

The most common prehistoric sites found in the area were
quarries for the procurement of chert, the best raw material for lithic
tool manufacture found locally. Another common site type is the lithic
workshop/campsite. These sites differ from the quarries in that the
debitage represents the later stages of the lithic reduction process.
Such artifacts as scrapers, bifaces, awls, choppers, knife and point
fragments and features such as hearths, may be present in this type
of site. Snow Camp Meadow is known to have been a place where
the gathering and possibly the preparation of brodelia and camas took
place.

The historic period of this area began in the 1790s when explorers and traders appeared in southwest Oregon. Some of the first permanent Euroamerican settlers in the area were miners attracted to the region during the gold rush era of the mid-1850s. Gold was first discovered on the coast at places like Gold Beach, named for the gold rich, black sand deposits found there. Later, gold deposits were found in the Rogue River. Early prospectors left little of the local country unexplored in their search for precious metals.

Following and accompanying the miners were the early settlers farming in the flat surrounding hills. An example of an early homestead in the area is the Windy Valley Homestead on Windy Creek, approximately two miles southeast of Snow Camp. This homestead site was first filed on in 1910 and a patent for the property was issued to Herman F. Jantzen in 1917. The original survey maps show that in 1916, the property had two separate houses, a barn, a smokehouse and a large frame structure near the cultivated area. It is Mr. Jantzen which gave Windy Valley its name. Apparently this was in reference to his love of talk and most people called him "Windy."

The survey notes made on his homestead listed these improvements:

A hewed log house, 26' x 34'	$ 425.
Log and shake house, 12' x 20'	75.
Shake barn, 10' x 20'	65.
Frame for barn of hewed logs, 42' x 52'	150.
Shake smoke house, 8' x 8'	20.
87 fruit trees	435.
Three and three-quarter acres under cultivation, surrounded by 140 rods of high picket fence	196.
Total value	$1,366.

That is a tremendous amount of work for one man. Unfortunately, all of the fruit trees and buildings are gone today. The property changed hands a number of times before being acquired by the US Government in 1974. A trail leads from the bottom of the hill just below Snow Camp Lookout through Windy Valley.

Development and growth continued as the settlers and their descendants utilized the area's abundant resources. During the late 19th and early 20th centuries, subsistence living occupied the largest portion of the population in southern Curry County. Canneries were established to take advantage of the prolific salmon runs, the lily bulb industry developed in the area's mild climate, and logging utilized the area's rich timber resource.

With the establishment of the Redwood Ranger District in 1909 as part of the Siskiyou National Forest, various trails, lookouts and telephone line were constructed in the general area. Trail systems connected Forest Service facilities, often following older aboriginal routes along the populated coastal and river areas

Snow Camp Lookout began as a "rag camp" in 1917–18 (during World War I), which was a semipermanent lookout site consisting of a tent camp, alidade (for pinpointing fires) and a telephone. A structure was first built in 1924 which was replaced with the present structure in 1958. During World War II, Snow Camp was staffed as an early warning post for spotting enemy aircraft. Many lookouts were used this way. Usually they were staffed with two people, often a married couple who took turns with twelve hour shifts. The last year Snow Camp saw regular service was 1972 until its reopening in 1990 as a recreation rental.

INSIDE OF LOOKOUT

"He who lives in glass house has lots of windows to wash."

SNOW CAMP JOURNAL — 1995

June 23 - Mother, Father, Jason, Lissa and Kim S.; Grants Pass, OR

(Father) Started vacation with two nights at Packer's Cabin. Very quiet, solitary spot where weather went from poor to beautiful.

Left there for Ludlum House. It looked beautiful on arrival...looked forward to fishing. Upon closer inspection, not very homey...no bunks, lots of mosquitoes and a rat. Upon seeing rat, decided to sleep outside. Kids saw a fox out in yard in the middle of the night. Woke to everyone whining about itching bites. Almost went home but instead found we could spend night here.

Glad we did...much more comfortable and clean. Outstanding view! Sunset, stars, sunrise. Did as many before us...watched sunrise, then back to sleep. Awoke very warm. Have to hurry up and go back. Vacation is over. Too bad. Looking forward to shower though!

Oh yeah...saw a bear yesterday.

I love this rental program and look forward to using it again. Thank you.

(Jason, age 15) We saw a bear cub on the way up here. It was cool. I was asleep.

(Mother) We stayed at Packer's Cabin, then Ludlum House. This is by far the best place I have ever stayed my whole life and I am old. We have two girls younger than Jason. They have probably gone up and down this hill seven times. Very beautiful. No words to describe such a magnificent view.

(Lissa, age 13) I had a lot of fun. It was very windy. We saw a bear. The bear was cool.

June 24 - Don and Carole S.; Rockford, WA

Our adventure began in January when I learned about Snow Camp Lookout. I immediately inquired and was able to reserve it for two days. Don was on fire lookouts, Bolivar (1955), and Bald Knob (1956), in the Powers Ranger District. This lookout trip was an anniversary present to him for our

35th anniversary. This was my first experience in a lookout and I have thoroughly enjoyed it. Don enjoyed the nostalgia of lookout life and the time to walk around and see things, as he couldn't do that when he was working.

June 26 - Marian D.; Benicia, CA

As we pack to leave, I try to soak up a little more of the view. I want to be able to close my eyes and be on this mountain top whenever and wherever I may be. The walk to Snow Camp Meadow is beautiful. An ideal walk in the early morning as you are protected from the wind and the sun. Four miles round trip. The sunsets were breathtaking. Vivid band of color lit up the sky for hours.

We had winds up to 70 mph at night. I didn't sleep but rather sailed through the sky dodging stars. I will never forget this place. I'll carry a piece of it with me always. Thank you God for showing me your face here on top of the world.

June 27 - Winnie H.; Antioch, CA

These past two days have been so spiritual. The wind blowing out all the stuck pieces in me from being a human doing instead of a human being. A reminder from a Higher power that beauty is all around us, if only we open our eyes.

June 27 and 28 - Dave and Linda; Crescent City, CA

Beautiful, serene, breathtaking, a piece of heaven not to be forgotten. A "time out" in a world moving so fast we forget to stop and see around us.

June 28 - JAS; Coquille, OR

The trip here was pretty uneventful, with exception of a flat tire. Once we made it through the gate however, things began to liven up. Someone must have spilled some food stuff in the wheelbarrow since it was being investigated by a pretty nice size black bear. We were able to drive within forty feet of the bruin before he decided to surrender his new found toy.

The pack up the hill was very energizing and really got the blood flowing, particularly from my knee wound I received when losing my footing the third trip up. The inside of the lookout was being guarded by a squadron of biting flies. The battle was furious and could have gone either way but in the end we were victorious. After a hearty meal and a fine Cuban cigar, nature was calling quite loudly (must have been the salsa). Much to my disgust, the outhouse has just a few more inches before overflowing; however, the view is spectacular.

During the night at about 0200, we were paid a visit by Mr. Bear. We had left one window open and managed to get it shut in time. He stood outside the door for several minutes before leaving us for the night. After that episode, having to deal with all the ants through the night seemed insignificant.

Good place to visit and we plan to return another time.

June 30 and 31 - Gene, Edith Ann, Misty and Jessop; Happy Camp, CA

Panther Lake is nothing more than a mud puddle but as hot as we were, we sat down in the middle of it.

Haven't seen that bear but I've heard that mouse called "Timothy."

July 2, 3, 4, and 5 - Debbie A., Greg and Jesse A.; Myrtle Creek, OR

We are hoping to see July 4th fireworks tonight. I'm afraid the coastal towns look pretty socked in with fog though.

July 5, 6 and 7 - Eric and Anne Rose P.; Eugene, OR

We drove up Wednesday after two nights in Packer's Cabin...whole trip is our honeymoon.

Eric has been to a couple of lookout towers further north in the Cascades and this is the most beautiful he's seen.

While at Packer's Cabin we hiked to Vulcan Lake (both), and that was a gorgeous swimming spot. Yesterday we took the walk to Snow Camp Meadow...also highly worth it. Lots of teeny wildflowers and zillions of those blue butterflies!

July 15 - Michael, Janet and Simon S.; Eugene, OR

(Michael) Rising moon stealing each mountain's edge...first one, then another. Such wind! The sky is amazing, I know so very little. Every four stars is the dipper. Snow Camp Lookout...firewatch vista offering emptiness, both miniature and vast, invites you to watch the world turn. Do nothing, be nothing.

(Janet) Major white water trip suddenly canceled due to too high volume water on Lower Salmon...couldn't believe our luck that someone canceled up here on twenty-four hours notice and we got called. One of the loveliest "top of the world" experiences I've ever had, and first time in a shelter that wouldn't blow away!

Great bright sun and cloudless days. Of course, the intense wind, leading us to believe we might be able to fly.... No visitors, bi or quadri. One hawk yesterday.

No picture could ever do this place justice.

July 16, 17 and 18 - Lewis; Central Point, OR

The horseflies are amazing. We are at times prisoners here. They dive-bomb the windows systematically looking for weakness. Together with the flying ants, mosquitoes and biting flies, they hover en masse outside the door.

Escaped long enough to go on a gruesome five mile hike. It about killed Dain (9), but to his credit he gutted it out. Returned to 90 degree cabin. Never has a glass of ice water tasted so fine.

The Milky Way is stunning; moonrise even more so. Had to sleep on wrong side because moon was so bright.

No sign of the bear or any other wildlife. The locked gate offers comfort, security against human intruders. Amazingly quiet, although the kids tend to disrupt things. I'm glad they got to enjoy staying up here but this place is much too romantic to bring kids. Next year we come alone.

July 20, 21 and 22 - Theresa and Jeff S.; Crescent City, CA

This is our second trip here. Out first was June 1994, our honeymoon. We spent our first night in Windy Valley.

It is rather strange. All around the fog is rising. To look out toward the ocean you would think we were on top of the world.

July 31 - Chas., Ann, Garret, Camerron and Madison; Bandon, OR

Been hiking these hills and swimming these rivers for nearly twenty years; never made it up here though. Now I can go in peace and rest in the serenity of my daydreams through binoculars spying on elk in Snow Camp Meadow or imagine soaring eagles over the Craggies.

We arrived mid-afternoon from Packer's Cabin and a dip in the Chetco. Drove the Mazda up to the door since we had Madison (10 months), and all her gear. Garret (14), and Cam (8) managed to stay busy arguing and swatting flies off the lizards in the underbrush.

August 4 and 5 - L. and M. B.; Grants Pass, OR

Here again. Much less wind than last year, only 35 mph.

I spent my "free" time working on the laptop computer we just got for a project due Tuesday. Not exactly what I'd hoped but it was either do it here or stay home. For awhile, I fancied myself a novelist up here getting great inspiration and writing the next best seller....

P.S. No ants, no bears, no flies...did we book the economy tour?

August 6, 7, 8 and 9 - Richard and Brother Bob; Brookings, OR

Wowee…the view, the wind, shooting stars (111), clouds, light, darkness, shadows…far out! Ten deer on the Game Lake road. Can see like in the desert. No bears, mice, ants, etc. Wood showed from USFS, thanks much.

Can see why limit of three days…could become addictive. Enjoyed the whole experience. Wind a little "iffee." Brother Bob starting to smell…a sure indication that it's time to go.

Extremely difficult getting the Winnebago turned around at the top. Had to disconnect trailer.

Rex was a good dog. Too bad he took out after that puma…well, it's all nature.

August 9, 10, 11, 12 and 13 - David C. and Barbara K.; Applegate and Grants Pass, OR

This is my fourth trip to Snow Camp. I sure do love this place. Arrived this afternoon and after I unloaded and arranged everything, I sat down to feed my face and read, first the newspaper, then the new (to me) 1995 entries in the Snow Camp journal.

Bought a new Quickclicker pencil on the way up here and I have been dying to try it out so I'm writing already.

Coming from the rat race down below, I find it hard to slow down. Seems like I always need to be doing something. I remember the uneasiness I feel now and have felt on past visits here, that initial worry of being bored or not having enough to do. I also know that the feeling passes after a bit and with practice, I can get right into the "relaxing" mode. Occasional bouts of activity do overwhelm me, alas.

(August 9, 9 P.M.) Got restless so went for a ride on my four wheeler. Saw a herd of elk in Fairview Meadow and shot about twelve frames on my camera. Three bulls and maybe twelve to fifteen cows. As it was late, the light was marginal, but maybe I got a few good ones. Such magnificent animals.

(August 10) The screens on the windows are a great improvement, not that I need them today as it is cold and raining. I even have a fire going. Wait a minute, let me check the date. Yes, I wrote down August 10, but perhaps I was mistaken.

On two of my past visits here, I brought my faithful dog (a Doberman), "Vinnie." Such a great companion, so mellow, not at all like his breed's reputation is made out to be. More human than some "humans" I've known. What made me think of him was a journal entry referring to the dive-bombing horseflies. Vinnie would "guard" you as you were sunbathing by leaping after attacking horseflies. The resulting dust storm he would create made a solar shower more of a necessity than a luxury. If the horse fly would land somewhere out of reach, Vinnie would go into the staring mode, perhaps thinking shear brainpower would bring the horsefly down. Vinnie seemed to think, "If I affix my eyes upon him with enough intensity, surely I'll hypnotize him and that annoying fly will just come straight to me."

Vinnie died this spring and I miss him so. His endearing personality left a number of human mourners and many animal ones also, I'm sure.

(August 11, 10 A.M.) Woke this morning to clear skies and a brisk 15 mph wind from the east. I notice how most people become very aware of the weather when they are here. A great number of the journal entries deal with their observations on the wind, fog, rain, heat, etc. I think it is because: weather is more pronounced up here; it affects the visitor more because if it is unfavorable, they are confined to a 14' X 14' room; there are few diversions such as television, telephone or a trip to the corner store; it is hard to ignore wind so strong that you're afraid the lookout will go airborne any moment; or they are just plain bored.

The wind gauge is really nice. No more guessing as to how strong those gusts really are.

It appears that the USFS or volunteers did some major work here since the last paying guest (which was myself), was here in 1994. The decking all around the lookout has been replaced. The southwest corner has been "rebuilt." There were ants living there causing some serious damage. Screens on the windows, and the toilet floor no longer makes me worry about falling through. THANKS!

(August 13) I'm no longer alone as Barbara came up with her brother and his lady. They left yesterday morning leaving us together again.

By shuttling my truck around to the Windy Valley trailhead beforehand, we had a nice five mile hike from the lookout, through Windy Valley and to the road, mostly downhill. Windy Creek is about half way through. For anyone who does it this way, shortly after you cross the creek, the trail forks. To the right is the trailhead, to the left is the Windy Valley Meadow, maybe a third of a mile in. Very, very nice. The fork is not very well marked but the trail is obvious if you pay attention.

Last night the wind really blew. Thirty-five to 40 mph is "cookin'!"

We skied into Warner Mountain Lookout (outside Oakridge, OR) this spring for three days. A beautiful experience and a **very** nice lookout. Plan to try a newly opened/restored one called Little Mount Hoffman (outside McCloud, CA), soon. I suppose you could call me a "lookout junkie."

My love and I are off to the Illinois River. Isn't life just grand!

(Barbara) Almost let the hustle and bustle of every day "doing" instead of "being" keep me from a few days of reconnection here at Snow Camp. David's idea was perfect. We invited my brother and his friend up for the end of the Snow Camp rental period and he delivered me to my love. Hadn't done anything with my brother like camping in over twenty years! It was great to introduce them to the lookout experience. As David (admitted lookout junkie) pointed out, "The first night is free." We had a fun visit, listened to many stories and had a yummy late night meal on a moonlit Friday night.

Saturday, we hung around and helped them plan their escape to a camp in the trees somewhere lower down the mountain. David and I got a late start for our hike to Windy Valley. I was so moved by the constant changing beauty. We enjoyed shooting some photos and took some time to really commune with mom nature. We were serenaded by five buzzards and their music of wind and feathers overhead. They even were so kind to leave us one beautiful feather right there in the middle of the trail. Want to spend more time, hopefully, next year in the meadow and locate the old homestead.

Back for a hot solar shower with the help of adding boiling water to the bag. A nice dinner, foot soak and rub. Huge melon colored waning moon and lots of wind.

Sunday morning was tea and pumpkin muffins in bed. And visitors. Turned out to be two friendly genuine lookout junkies.

"Timothy" just got busted inside the garbage bag. He ran out in a big hurry...hope he got a little nourishment overnight.

(David) Although our two visitors had never stayed in a lookout, they had visited and taken pictures of an amazing eighty-five lookouts in seven years! They even had their photo album with them. So, Chris V., Coos Bay, OR, and Michael D., Springfield, OR, I salute you and I admire your hobby.

August 17 - Jeanie; Coburg, OR

This is our second visit to Snow Camp. My total of eleven days this year on lookouts (also at Indian Ridge up the McKenzie), really brings me "home."

The wonderful fireplace now in the Fairview Meadow/Enchanted Forest built by friends and family of Lane Lawson is quite a tribute to the man. Also makes me want to join them there sometime to share stories and a dinner with song.

August 18, 19 and 20 - Don, Alex, and Cole S., and Fran G.; Cottage Grove, OR

Spotted a fire on August 20 in the morning. Looks to be in the Babyfoot area.

"Tim," the mouse, made a visit on our first night. After reading the journal, we would have felt left out if he hadn't shown. Not to worry, only stayed and nibbled in the woodbox.

September 1, 2 and 3 - Dale, Michelle, Patrick (7) and Abigail (9) H.; Reedsport, OR

(Dale) We have decided an appropriate addition would be to leave the Phillips Plainisphere Star map. Without it my knowledge of the sky would be minimal.

The children set about picking up glass bits, gun shells and even the pieces of an old boot. They enjoyed hearing a reading of other occupants as chronicled herein.

The wind has picked up and a jacket is required but there always seems to be one side of the cabin, on the deck, that allows protection and I sit now facing the west with the sun a few hours from setting, shining out over the nacreous sea.

So we are privileged to spend a few nights on the pinnacle before we return to the gas powered flatlands. But the mountain has only one peak and many sides, the journey as important as its end. So through the next month or years or longer, I will try to look at nature's beauty and bounty more often, for the years slip by all too quickly.

If my words did glow with the gold of sunshine,
And my tunes were played on the harp unstrung,
Would you hear my voice come through the music?
Would you hold it close as it were your own?
It's a hand-me-down, the thoughts are broken.
Perhaps they're better left unsung,
I don't know, don't really care,
Let there be songs to fill the air.
Ripple in still water when there is no pebble cast or wind to blow;
Reach out your hand if your cup is empty,
If your cup is full may it be again.
Let it be known there is a fountain,
That was not built by the hands of man...

Hunter/Garcia

I think of you still, Mr. Jerry Garcia, a man I never met but had great influence on my life. August 2, 1942–August 9, 1995.

September 11 - Joan and Larry; Eugene, OR

This was our fourth visit and by far the laziest! After a too busy summer and before fall activities begin, we decided to really relax (easy for Larry but a real challenge for me). We planned our stay around the full moon which added to the romance of it all. We napped, wrote letters, showered, ate and repeated it all over again. Our longest hike was down the hill to our van to get supplies.

September 14, 15, 16 and 17 - Torrie and Bob; Salem, OR

One of the wonderful things about returning to Snow Camp for this, our third visit, is to see the additions since our last visit (the sign, the deck and…WOW…the screens!) Thank you!

Our visit this year is calmer than years past…fall rhythms I think. We are content to watch the fog fill the valleys, cascading over ridges, rising and falling but never quite reaching us.

September 20 - Graig and Barbara D.; Cave Junction, OR

Third time is a charm. No visitors, great weather, no snafus. Great time. This year we brought a radio. It's amazing what you can pick up…Los Angles to Seattle (almost). Listened to some news and radio dramas.

Compared to previous years, this has been a pretty uneventful trip. No state police dropping in, no lightning storms, no visits from Forest Service law enforcement, no bear hunters dropping by. Just peace and quiet (and the wind).

A compliment to all the Snow Camp residents. Everyone seems to be literate, thoughtful and very caring about this place. For us, this isn't just a motel room on top of a mountain, it's a special retreat. Thanks.

September 20 and 21 - Jean M. and Larry S.; Grants Pass and Trail, OR; also Judith K. and Richard E.; Jacksonville, OR

(Jean) Renewal…this wonderful place helps one to continue on life's journey. We move, we camp, we move again and hope to visit other lookouts.

(Larry) After reading about this place in a magazine, I mentioned it to some friends in the spring and we decided to give it a try. Would you believe there were no weekends available? I would, now that I've been here! September 20th and 21st were the first two days together so I grabbed them.

The drive over from the Rogue Valley was uneventful but the lookout fulfilled all our expectations. I could get to be a "lookout junkie" real easy. Wow! The view, the serenity, the place!

Hauling water up the hill is a killer but that will tend to keep the "deadbeats" away. I camp constantly and almost every campsite I've found that is easily accessible is soon a littered mess from those too lazy to clean up after themselves. From the looks of this place when we arrived, it's used by a better class of camper. I pray it stays that way.

P.S. I highly recommend the swimming hole below the bridge on the Chetco River!

(Judith) We stayed here with Larry and Jean. It's been a lovely stay and a nice ending to the year. I often try to spend the last days of the year in special places, secluded and thought provoking. It is the time when my clock says to slow down and turn inward to face the winter months and short days. No more hiking for awhile till the snow falls and we can take out the cross-country skis.

(Richard) In this spot many have looked out only to see a different view, for it is in each person that the picture has meaning. Here there is peace for the traveler, with only the bold open space of nature to remind you that life is so precious. The universe wants all to be happy. Today I am.

September 22, 23 and 24 - Marcy M. and Kent H.; Eureka, CA

Our second trip to Snow Camp. We just kind of walk around giggling about how smart...lucky...blessed we are to come here. Our friends Cheryl and Russ joined us Friday.

Just as we were relaxing Friday late afternoon, we heard a car and dogs barking. We were quite shocked to find an old truck with two older gents and three Walker hounds parked by our cars! I didn't quite follow their logic but their story was something about the young fella with them had gone down the Windy Valley trail to try to find their lost dogs. The dogs had radio tracking collars on. I asked how they got in and the one man—the one with the BIG belly, bad limp and chewing tobacco dripping down his chin—said that the young fella works for the Forest Service. We returned to the lookout; they left sometime later, though we heard the dogs intermittently all night.

Perfect evening, sunset from no colors in **my** crayon set. So still and quiet that my ears would pulse. No moon, so the stars were incredible. We want to make up our own constellation myths: Harley Davidson rider, Susan's computer mouse...we hardly slept for the night show (and then there was Kent's snoring).

So now it's Saturday morning and Cheryl and Russ have to leave. Five minutes later they are walking back up the hill. They are locked in!! It seems that the dog-men, instead of just locking the combo lock, didn't know enough about what they were doing and locked the padlock too.

Cheryl and Russ sat by the road for two hours before a hunter came by. He couldn't take them anywhere but he knew where there was someone camped with a cellular phone. The ranger unlocked the gate a few hours later. Ranger was very interested in the dog-men because the dogs are used primarily to hunt bear and that's illegal now. And to have a Forest Service employee with them, well now, that's just downright interesting.

Today is the first day of Fall. Time to reap what we have sown.

September 29 - Glenn and Linda T.; Gold Beach, OR
AAH!

October 3 - Wayne and Carol R.; Medford, OR
Another great time!

How do you keep people out. One person came up Sunday, then two others. They were here at least an hour taking pictures.

Remember, there is no such thing as "bad" weather. Easier to suffer inclemency rather than the fools who trudge up here expecting to be warmly greeted…!

October 8 - Julie and Emily C.; Portland, OR
(Julie) Spirited my twelve year old out of school and headed south. Directions from Forest Service were excellent…no problems in the dark, memories along the mountain dirt roads of living in the Greensprings, planting trees, long visits with neighbors over coffee and kitchen sink soup. Got to the gate at quarter to ten P.M. and my brain power had apparently evaporated because, though I worked the combo lock off, I couldn't fathom how to disengage the caboodle. Woke up Em and she good-naturedly grabbed bedding and we walked the road up. Nearly blown off the stairway, each venture outside a moonlit, foot free adventure. We settled in.

By the morning, the wind had quieted a lot and we discovered the wind gauge, then 40-55 mph. Sun broke entirely through and beautiful fall; calm, walking, cards, reading and eating. By this time Emily had sorted out both the gate and the wheelbarrow and we were up the road and **up** the road and **up** the road. I like the rhythm of "OK, what's next?"

(Emily) today we tried very unsuccessfully to mop the floor, but as some of you might find soon, it did not work very well. So we tried the Pippi Longstockings technique, sliding around with paper towels on our feet.

This morning when I woke up, I took some pictures of sunrise and then took a walk— destination Port-O-Potty.

October 10 - Gretchen H. (13); Eugene, OR

Yesterday I tried forever to fix the kite somebody left here so it would fly, but it just flopped around, two feet off the ground.

Hey! Why didn't someone tell us about the outhouse just to the west? We'd been going all the way down to the one by the trailhead and parking spot. Sure, we saw that weird green building, but who would have guessed it was another outhouse.

The nicest thing about being here with only family is that I haven't washed my hair for three days and nobody cares! Ha! I want to live up here.

October 11 and 12 - Kim and Paula H.; Salem, OR

(Paula) I was interested and slightly amused by the comments from the couple from Philadelphia who were surprised to have hikers come to the lookout. We who have been hiking in Oregon for many years frequently have, and have had a lookout as a destination, "manned" or empty. Usually it has been someone on fire-watch, but not always. We've always respected their wishes and their privacy if they request, but we do stay around and enjoy the view for a while. I would suggest…not that you put a sign at the parking lot about renters (as you have at the gate), but that you make a notation in the information you give to renters that hikers may come up to the lookout and that those renting have the right to welcome them into the building, or not, as they wish. The land is USFS, the cabin is rented. It is just a matter of everyone understanding what is acceptable.

October 22 - Zeke and Lora R.; Brookings, OR

The painters have arrived! We had three glorious days here, painted window frames inside and the fascia board outside. We really enjoyed Snow Camp and would not mind coming back to do more work on the place.

Did a lot of daydreaming about living here. Now it is time to go but we don't want to.

That was the last entry for Snow Camp's 1995 season.

*In June of 1996, the story will
continue with your journal entries.*

SIGN AT JUNCTION LEAVING SNOW CAMP LOOKOUT

SNOW CAMP MEADOW

HIKING OPPORTUNITIES AROUND SNOW CAMP LOOKOUT

     Several beautiful natural areas lie within hiking distance of the lookout. The bare, red soils predominant in this area are derived from the ultrabasic mineral serpentine and supports a unique ecosystem. Look for wildlife and wildflowers, cool off in Windy Creek, or take a quiet walk through the "Enchanted Forest."

     Snow Camp Meadow is a large natural meadow visible only from outside the lookout (from the mountaintop, about 200 feet north of the lookout). To hike there, take the trail down from the parking area (it will appear at first that you are headed in the wrong direction), and turn right at the junction, or hike in from Forest Service Road 360. Elk, bear, blue grouse and other wildlife frequent the meadow. Look for western tree frogs and caddis flies in the pond. Enjoy the multitude of wildflowers, but please do not pick them.

     Fairview Meadow and the "Enchanted Forest" are located north of the lookout and you will pass between them traveling Forest Service Road 3680. Meadows like Fairview were probably created when burnt by the Native Americans and early settlers. They provide habitat for wildlife and support rare plants not found in the forested environment. The "Enchanted Forest" is a hauntingly beautiful stand of old-growth Douglas fir. The trees are so dense that there is little or no undergrowth. Look for the unusual "candelabra" shaped trees amidst the crowded trunks. The lichen hanging from the trees, known as old man's beard, take all of their nutrients and water from the air— a testament to the high rainfall here.

     Windy Valley lies more than 1000 feet below and southwest of Snow Camp Lookout. This is the site of a homestead created after the turn of the century by Herman Jantzen (also known as "Windy"), and is a great place to spend an afternoon. Take the trail down (south), from the parking area and turn left at the trail junction, on the ridge south of the lookout. From this trail you can also access Panther Lake, a seasonal pond. The trail is steep, so be sure to have plenty of time, and take adequate drinking water. If you desire, just as you cross Windy Creek, turn right and continue on the trail that comes out on Forest Service Road 1376. If you turn left after crossing the creek, another one-third mile will bring you to a beautiful meadow where Windy's homestead once was.

WITHIN AN HOUR'S DRIVE of Snow Camp Lookout are many opportunities for exploration and recreation. Some of the more popular choices are:

Game Lake which is located approximately eleven miles northeast of Snow Camp Lookout at the end of Forest Service Road 400. It is a popular spot to visit and the departure point for several trails including one into the Kalmiopsis Wilderness.

Tincup and Upper Chetco Trails are located approximately ten miles southeast of Snow Camp Lookout at the end of Forest Service Road 360 (off of Forest Service Road 1376). These trails access the Kalmiopsis Wilderness, a rugged and steep land where you can find solitude, pristine wilderness and challenging backcountry hiking.

Quail Prairie and Long Ridge are located southeast of Snow Camp Lookout on Forest Service Road 1917. Quail Prairie Lookout is still in operation and welcomes visitors. Historic Packer's Cabin off of Long Ridge is available to rent through the Chetco Ranger District in Brookings.

The Chetco Wild and Scenic River parallels the road from Brookings (Forest Service Road 1376). A more pristine river would be hard to find. Along it you will find opportunities for float trips, fishing, camping and swimming.

The Kalmiopsis Wilderness Area consists of 179,850 acres and was established in 1964 under the Wilderness Act. As early as 1946 it was identified as a Primitive or Wild Area. Except for primitive trails, there are no recreational developments or improvements in the Wilderness Area. This a harsh, rugged country with a character much different from that of most wilderness areas. It is a land of rocky, brushy, low elevation canyons rather than a land of lofty peaks and long distance views. In spite of its harshness, or perhaps because of it, the area has a unique beauty and fascination.

Bontanicly, the Kalmiopsis Wilderness and the territory surrounding it is perhaps the most interesting region in the Northwestern United States. The serpentine soil supports several rare plants, some of which are considered sensitive and are protected by state and federal law. The *Kalmiopsis leachiana,* a small shrub somewhat resembling a miniature rhododendron, is a relic of the pre-ice age. Another is the flycatcher plant *(Darlingtonia californica)*, which is found in some wet areas. Keep a watch out for the attractive Bolander's Lily *(Lilium bolanderi).* It is deep wine red in color, turning yellow toward the center with maroon colored dots extending to the tip. They bloom June to July and are found only on rocky serpentine slopes in the Siskiyou Mountains of southwest Oregon.

Also, over 12 species of coniferous trees, 9 species of hardwood trees, 31 species of shrubs and many species of herbaceous plants are found here. To help you identify these plants, it is suggested you bring a field guide such as one of the Audubon Society field guide books or *Key Species for Plant Identification on the Rogue River, Siskiyou and Umpqua National Forests*. They are usually available at the Gold Beach Ranger District Visitors' Center, 1225 S. Ellensburg, Gold Beach, OR 97444, (541) 247-3600. Or contact other national forest offices in southern Oregon. Enjoy these special plants and the beautiful flowers, but *please* leave them to grow in their natural environment. Their future may depend on it.

Shortly after gold was discovered in southern Oregon in 1851, the stream bottoms in the head of the Chetco River were found to be rich. The history of the early mining activity is meager. It is known that many miners, including large numbers of Chinese, were employed in the area that is now classified as Wilderness. The rich placers and lodes were soon exhausted and mining activity dropped to a few old prospectors who made their homes in the upper Chetco and eked out a meager living hunting "pockets" and panning creek gravel. With World War II came a great need for chromium, and once again fever-ish activity developed.

Visitors to the Wilderness will note numerous roads in the east-ern or southwestern portions. These roads were constructed by miners as access to valid mining claims. They were built mostly during and immediately after World War II when stockpiling of chrome ores was important to the nation. These roads are closed by locked gates. With the termination of the Government stockpile program, chrome mining ceased abruptly. Remnants of the buildings and equipment along with large strips of land laid bare still remain in the Wilderness.

Additional information about the Kalmiopsis Wilderness Area can be obtained from the Chetco Ranger District, 555 Fifth Street, Brookings, OR 97415, (541) 469-2196 or the Siskiyou National Forest Headquarters, PO Box 440, Grants Pass, OR 97526, (541) 471-6500.

Darlingtonia californica
Pitcher plant

Modified hollow leaves trap
and digest insects for nutrients.

Kalmiopsis leachiana

A small shrub somewhat resembling a miniature rhododendron

Lilium bolanderi
Bolander's lily

Crimson flowers, petals slightly
recurved, open stony hillsides.

AFTERWORD

Snow Camp Lookout represents more than just an era gone by and a one-of-a-kind motel room. It symbolizes a return to a simpler place and time, especially pertinent in this fast paced world which most of us wish we could escape from, if only for a day or two. A night at Snow Camp gives people a chance to retreat to a sanctuary far away from the television, telephone, noise, traffic and chaos of daily life. As the human population increases and nature decreases, special places like Snow Camp are becoming harder to find and infinitely more precious.

Just a few decades ago, it was the policy of our government agencies to destroy unused cabins, guard stations and lookouts located on public land. They disappeared from the forests by the thousands, leaving few traces of their former existence. This was a shortsighted policy designed to keep squatters from utilizing them or just to eliminate a "safety hazard." But by the late 1980s, the value of these unique places began to be recognized. Through the sustained voices of a few visionaries in the Forest Service, combined with the efforts of dedicated volunteers, some of these remote retreats were renovated and made available to the public. As of this writing, about forty lookouts are available to rent in the western United States (see Appendix). There are some fire lookouts that still see regular service and a few others remain that are in dire need of renovation. But of the 5,060 fire lookouts which once dotted America, what remains is a small number indeed. Hopefully, the remaining facilities that survive will get the attention they deserve so that they too will see and hear new life again.

In the six years since Snow Camp Lookout was revived, a number of fortunate people were able to spend some time there and many returned year after year to renew themselves. I think the unique adventure of staying in "a glass house on top of the world" has a profound effect on most of the guests. The journal provided the opportunity for each guest to write their personal feelings about this awe inspiring experience. The poets, artists, writers and storytellers were given free rein and expressed themselves in a variety of ways. As one reads the numerous journal entries, a slice of the marvelous human drama that unfolds on Snow Camp Mountain is revealed. You see relationships blossom and renew, anniversaries celebrated, babies conceived and an awareness of all life brought forth. Not only do people slow down and become more conscious of their surroundings but some have taken a bit of that serenity back home with them. Perhaps that time on the mountain fostered a good deed or kind word, which was contagious, causing another to do the same.

Much is revealed when a common mouse dubbed "Timothy" shows himself to the cabin's occupants. At home, one would probably not think twice about employing some means of dispatching a similar mouse. But at Snow Camp, a unique personality emerges. Perhaps that tolerance for another living creature is due to reading the journal entries or maybe it is the influence of the spectacular surroundings. I believe Mother Nature evokes a powerful voice in the spirit of all humankind and though some choose not to hear, the voice still whispers.

AUTHOR'S NOTE

Fire once was a natural phenomenon that occurred regularly in a healthy forest. It performed a periodic cleansing by reducing the undergrowth, germinating seeds and leaving the strongest trees to survive and reproduce. Although man had good intentions when he sought to deny fire in the forest for the last eight decades, his interference has had devastating effects. One result is an overstocking of tree stands which can lead to catastrophic fires or epidemic insect infestations. When a fire starts, whether by man or lightning, millions of dollars are spent on manpower and equipment for containment. Allowing a fire to follow its natural course is unlikely when so many of our homes are dispersed in the forests. Prevention may be the key. One school of thought is to mimic fire through logging practices. Another approach would be to introduce controlled burns when weather conditions are conducive. It is time to rethink our policy on suppressing all fires and consider whether Mother Nature knows best.

APPENDIX

•

Maps of Snow Camp Lookout Area

•

Directions to Snow Camp Lookout

•

List of Things to Take With You

•

List of Lookout Rentals Available
in the Western United States

•

The Lookout Experience

•

About the Author

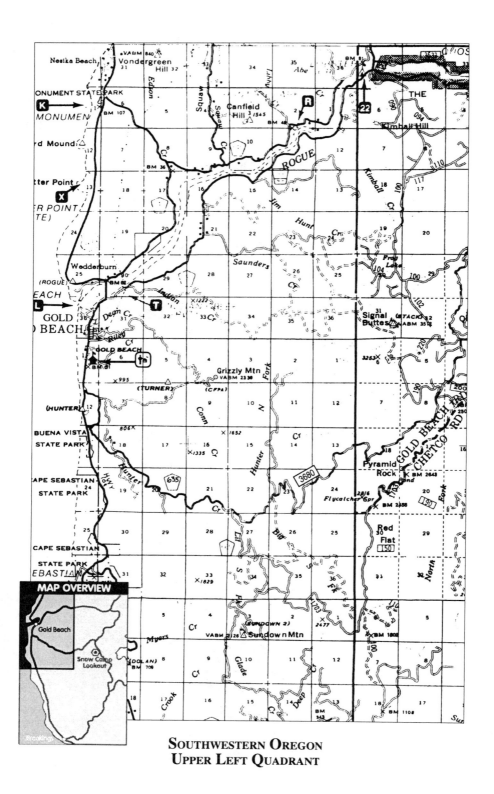

SOUTHWESTERN OREGON
UPPER LEFT QUADRANT

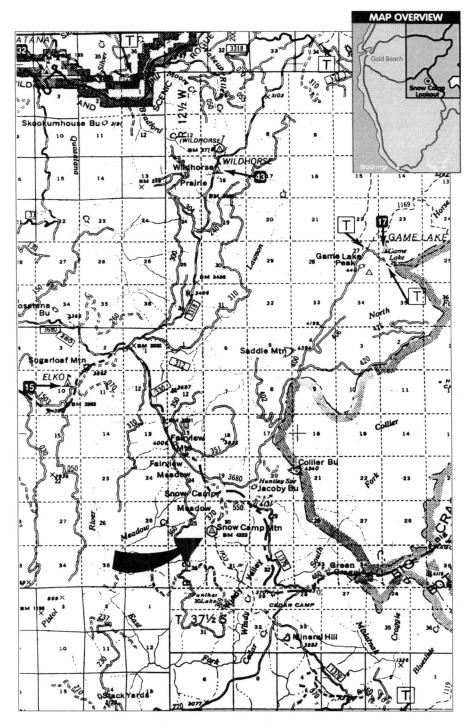

SOUTHWESTERN OREGON
UPPER RIGHT QUADRANT

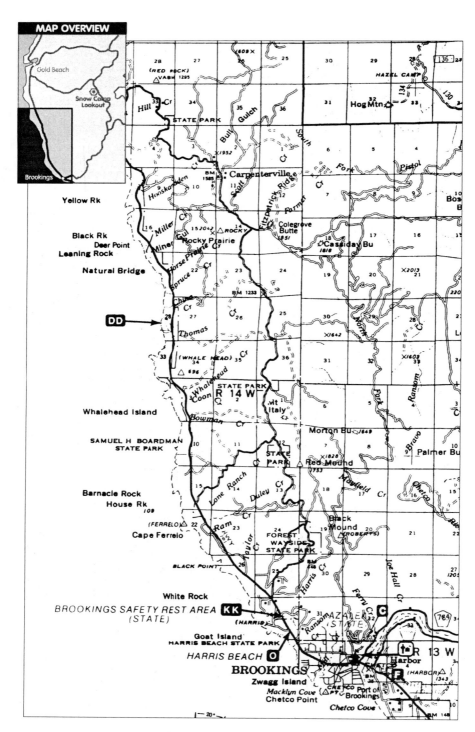

MAP OVERVIEW

Gold Beach

Snow Camp
Lookout

Brookings

Yellow Rk

Black Rk
Deer Point
Leaning Rock

Natural Bridge

DD

Whalehead Island

SAMUEL H BOARDMAN
STATE PARK

Barnacle Rock
House Rk
109

Cape Ferrelo

BLACK POINT

White Rock

BROOKINGS SAFETY REST AREA
(STATE)

Goat Island
HARRIS BEACH STATE PARK

HARRIS BEACH

BROOKINGS

Zwagg Island
Macklun Cove
Chetco Point

(RED ROCK)
VABM 1295

Hill Cr STATE PARK

Carpenterville
BM 1585

Honskarden

Miller Cr

Rocky Prairie
Miner Cr

Horse Prairie Cr

Spruce Cr

Chine Cr

Thomas

(WHALE HEAD)
34

Whalehead

Coon
Bowman Cr

Lone Ranch Cr

Duley Cr

Ram Cr

Taylor Cr

(FERRELO)

(HARRIS)

HAZEL CAMP

Hog Mtn

South Fork

Fitzpatrick Ridge

Colegrove
Butte
1851

Cassiday Bu
1818

BM 1233

STATE PARK
R 14 W

Mt
Italy

Morton Bu J649

STATE
PARK
Red Mound
1753

Mansfield Cr

Black
Mound
(ROBERTS)

FOREST
WAYSIDE
STATE PARK

BM

Harris Cr

KK

Ransom Cr

AZALEA
STATE

C

R 13 W

Harbor
(HARBOR)
1343

CHETCO Port of
Brookings

Chetco Cove

Pistol

Bos
B

X2013

North Fork

Ransom

Park

Palmer Bu

Chetco

Joe Hall Cr

789

BM 148

**SOUTHWESTERN OREGON
LOWER LEFT QUADRANT**

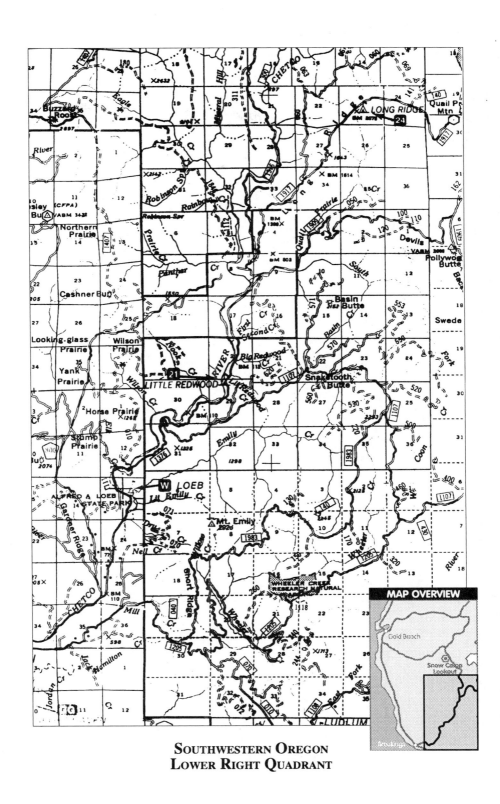

SOUTHWESTERN OREGON
LOWER RIGHT QUADRANT

MAP OVERVIEW

DIRECTIONS TO SNOW CAMP LOOKOUT

The lookout may be reached by a southern route, a northern route or an inland route over the mountains.

From the south

If you are coming from the south on Highway 101, just as you enter Brookings turn northeast (right), onto the North Bank Chetco River road (County road #784). Follow the signs to Loeb State Park. The road becomes a single lane with turnouts. It turns into Forest Service road #1376, a gravel surface. Stay on #1376 for 25.4 miles from Loeb, until you reach a fork at Forest Service road #550, which is marked "Snow Camp Lookout" to the left. About one mile further you will see a locked gate to Snow Camp Lookout . Your confirmation letter will have given you the combination to the lock. You have another half mile to go. The parking lot at the base of "the hill" is still two hundred yards short of the lookout.

From the north

If you are coming from the north on Highway 101, about two miles south of Gold Beach, turn southeast (left), onto Hunter Creek road (County road #635). After several miles the pavement ends and becomes Forest Service road #3680, a gravel surface. Stay on #3680 for approximately twenty-two miles until it forks into Forest Service road #1376. Forest Service road #590 is about two miles down #1376. Proceed through the locked gate using the combination written on your confirmation letter. It is another half mile to the parking lot at the base of "the hill."

From inland or I-5

If you are coming from inland, turn west at the Merlin exit off of I-5, north of Grants Pass. Proceed through Merlin which will eventually take you along the Rogue River. Just short of Galice turn west (left), onto Forest Service road #23. This is a narrow, winding, paved mountain road with turnouts. In the summer months, there is considerable traffic. Drive carefully. Stay on Forest Service road #23 until it again joins the Rogue River. Turn left and proceed approximately ten miles down the Rogue River on Forest Service road #33 which is a paved two lane road. Turn south (left), on Forest Service road #3318. Go approximately fourteen miles and turn left onto Forest Service road #1376. Follow the signs to Snow Camp Lookout.

To insure your privacy while staying at Snow Camp, feel free to lock the gate on the access road which is one half mile before the lookout. Visitors may still walk in, but any drive-in visitors should be on official business. You have the right to deny walk-in visitors access to the interior of the lookout if you so desire, as you are renting the facility; however, the outside area is public domain.

LIST OF THINGS TO TAKE WITH YOU

Basic Items:
Bedding and/or sleeping bags
Pillow
Camera and film
Binoculars or telescope
Ice chest and ice
Maps
Portable radio
Flashlights and batteries
Backpack or fanny pack for hiking
Water (very important)
Lantern, fuel and extra mantles
Candles (when all else fails)
Gas stove and fuel
Matches
Can opener
Dish towel
Dish soap
Sharp knife
Garbage bags (pack it in, pack it out)
Toilet paper
Paper towels
Salt, pepper and spices
Cooking oil
Food and condiments
Coffee or tea
Air mattress (if more than two people)
First aid kit
Tool kit (for repairs)

Personal Items:
Tooth brush and tooth paste
Sun screen and sunglasses
Hat
Hiking boots
Bug repellent
Rx Medications
Towel and wash cloth
Bar soap
Hair brush
Lotion
Lip balm
Eye glasses or contacts and
  saline
Rain gear
Clothes for all types of weather

Consider Taking:
Book
Games, cards or puzzle
Canteen
Compass
Swiss army knife
Snow Camp Lookout book
Solar shower
Rope – small diameter, nylon
Thermos for beverages

Snow Camp Lookout comes equipped with many basic cooking utensils such as pots, pans, dishes, silverware and a tea pot. These items have been donated and although not guaranteed to be there, I have always found enough to do the job. If you do bring some items, don't pack them up "the hill" until you do an inventory of what is already available in the lookout.

LOOKOUT RENTALS AVAILABLE IN THE WESTERN UNITED STATES

Name, Elevation, Fee	Contact	Available
Snow Camp Lookout Siskiyou National Forest 4,223 ft $30	Chetco Ranger District 555 Fifth Street Brookings, OR 97415 541-469-2196	May - Oct
Pearsoll Peak Lookout Siskiyou National Forest 5,098 ft	Illinois Ranger District 26568 Redwood Hwy Cave Junction, OR 97523 541-592-2166	Year around
Acker Rock Lookout Umpqua National Forest 4,112 ft $40	Tiller Ranger District 27812 Tiller-Trail Hwy Tiller, OR 97484 541-825-3201	June - Oct
Pickett Butte Lookout Umpqua National Forest 3,200 ft $40	Tiller Ranger District 27812 Tiller-Trail Hwy Tiller, OR 97484 541-825-3201	Nov - May
Hager Mountain Lookout Fremont National Forest 7,195 ft $25	Silver Lake Ranger District PO Box 129 Silver Lake, OR 97638 541-576-2107	Nov 1 - June 1
Bald Butte Lookout Fremont National Forest 7,536 ft $25	Paisley Ranger District PO Box 67 Paisley, OR 97636 541-943-3114	Year around
Flagtail Lookout Malheur National Forest 6,584 ft $25	Bear Valley Ranger District 528 E. Main Street John Day, OR 97845 541-575-3200	Nov 1 - May 31
Fall Mountain Lookout Malheur National Forest 5,949 ft $25	Bear Valley Ranger District 528 E. Main Street John Day, OR 97845 541-575-3200	Nov 1 - May 31
Five Mile Butte Lookout Mount Hood National Forest 4,627 ft $25	Barlow Ranger District PO Box 67 Dufur, OR 97021 541-467-2291	Nov 1 - May 31
Flag Point Lookout Mount Hood National Forest 5,650 ft $25	Barlow Ranger District PO Box 67 Dufur, OR 97021 541-467-2291	Nov 1 - May 31

Warner Mountain Lookout Willamette National Forest 5,800 ft $25 1st, $20 2nd	Rigdon Ranger District PO Box 1410 Oakridge, OR 97463 541-782-2283	Dec 1 - May 10
Indian Ridge Lookout Willamette National Forest 5,405 ft $20	Blue River Ranger District PO Box 199 Blue River, OR 97413 541-822-3317	June - Oct
Clearwater Lookout (Cabin) Umatilla Ranger District 5,600 ft $25	Pomeroy Ranger District Route 1, Box 53-F Pomeroy, WA 99347 509-843-1891	Year Around
Burley Mountain Lookout Gifford Pinchot Natl. Forest 5,310 ft $20	Randle Ranger District PO Box 670 Randle, WA 98377 306-497-1100	Nov 1 - May 31
Oak Flat Lookout Sequoia National Forest 4,900 ft $25	Greenhorn Ranger District PO Box 6129 Bakersfield, CA 93386 805-871-2223	Year Around
Little Mount Hoffman Shasta-Trinity National Forests 7,309 ft $35	McCloud Ranger District PO Box 1620 McCloud, CA 96057 916-964-2184	Year Around
Robbs Hut (Cabin) Eldorado National Forest 6,686 ft $35	Eldorado National Forest 3070 Camino Heights Drive Camino, CA 95709 916-644-6048	Year Around
Kloshe Nanitch Lookout Olympic National Forest 3,160 ft	Soleduck Ranger District 196281 Highway 101 Forks, WA 98331 360-374-6522	Projected opening in 1997
Summit Ridge Lookout (Cabin) Black Hills National Forest 5,662 ft $20	Elk Mountain Ranger District 1225 Washington Blvd. Newcastle, WY 82701 307-746-2782	Memorial Day - Labor Day
Jersey Jim Lookout San Juan National Forest 10,000 ft $45	Mancos Ranger District Jersey Jim Foundation PO Box 1032 Mancos, CO 81328 970-533-7060	Mid May - Late September

Clear Lake Butte Lookout Mount Hood National Forest 4,458 ft	Bear Springs Ranger Dist. Route 1, Box 222 Maupin, OR 97037 541-328-6211	Projected opening soon
Bishop Mountain Lookout Targhee National Forest 7,800 ft $15	Ashton Ranger District 228 Yellowstone Highway Ashton, ID 83420 208-652-7442	Year Around
McCart Lookout Bitterroot National Forest 7,115 ft $25	Sula Ranger District 7338 Highway 93 South Sula, MT 59871 406-821-3201	May 1 - Oct 30
Walde Mountain Lookout (Cabin) Clearwater National Forest 5,221 ft $15/day, Min 2 days.	Lochsa Ranger District #1 PO Box 398 Kooskia, ID 83539 208-926-4275	Jan 1 - Mar 31
Castle Butte Lookout (Cabin) Clearwater National Forest 6,659 ft $30/day, Min 2 days.	Lochsa Ranger District #1 PO Box 398, Kooskia, ID 83539 208-926-4275	July 15 - Sept 30
Austin Ridge Lookout Clearwater National Forest 4,731 ft $25/day, Min 2 days.	Pierce Ranger District Route 2, Box 191 Kamiah, ID 83536 208-935-2513	June 20 - Sept 15
Weitas Butte Lookout Clearwater National Forest 5,967 ft $25/day, Min 2 days.	Pierce Ranger District Route 2, Box 191 Kamiah, ID 83536 208-935-2513	July 15 - Sept 15
Wallow Mountain Lookout Clearwater National Forest 5,980 ft $30	North Fork Ranger District 1225 Ahsahka Road Orofino, ID 83544 208-476-3775	June 15 - Sept 1
Hornet Lookout (Cabin) Flathead National Forest 6,744 ft $15	Glacier View Ranger District 774 RR Street Columbia Falls, MT 59912 406-892-4372	Year Around
Garnet Mountain Lookout (Cabin) Gallatin National Forest 8,245 ft $25	Boseman Ranger District 3710 Fallon Street, Box C Boseman, MT 59715 406-587-6920	Dec 1 - Oct 15

167

Deer Ridge Lookout Idaho Panhandle National Forest 4,755 ft $25	Bonners Ferry Ranger Dist. Route 4, Box 4860 Bonners Ferry, ID 83805 208-267-5561	June 15 - Sept 30
Shorty Peak Lookout (Cabin) Idaho Panhandle National Forest 6,775 ft $20	Bonners Ferry Ranger Dist. Route 4, Box 4860 Bonners Ferry, ID 83805 208-267-5561	July 1 - Sept 30
Webb Mountain Lookout (Cabin) Kootenai National Forest 5,988 ft $20	Rexford Ranger District 1299 Hwy 93 N Eureka, MT 59917 406-296-2536	Year Around
McGuire Lookout (Cabin) Kootenai National Forest 6,986 ft $15	Rexford Ranger District 1299 Hwy 93 N Eureka, MT 59917 406-296-2536	Year Around
Big Creek Baldy Mountain Lookout Kootenai National Forest 5,768 ft $25	Libby Ranger District 12557 Highway 37 Libby, MT 59923 406-293-7773	June 1 - Oct 1
Gem Peak Lookout Kootenai National Forest 6,092 ft $25	Cabinet Ranger District 2693 Highway 200 Trout Creek, MT 59874 406-827-3533	June 1 - Nov 1
Sex Peak Lookout (Cabin) Kootenai National Forest 5,798 ft $25	Cabinet Ranger District 2693 Highway 200 Trout Creek, MT 59874 406-827-3533	Year Around
West Fork Butte Lookout (Cabin) Lolo National Forest 6,157 ft $15	Missoula Ranger District Bldg. 24A, Ft. Missoula Missoula, MT 59801 406-329-3814	Oct 1 - June 1
Priscilla Peak Lookout (Cabin) Lolo National Forest 7,004 ft $20	Plains Ranger District PO Box 674 Thompson Falls, MT 59873 406-827-3589	Year Around
Lookout Butte Lookout Nez Perce National Forest 5,869 ft $20	Selway Ranger District HCR75, Box 91 Kooskia, ID 83539 208-926-4258	June 15 - Sept 30

THE LOOKOUT EXPERIENCE

Be aware, renting a lookout or lookout cabin is not for everyone. This is a backwoods experience that can be downright rugged at times. Many of these lookouts are only available in the winter months; therefore getting to them may be an ordeal in itself. Even in the summer months, the weather at these elevations can change rapidly. A warm summer day can quickly turn cold and rainy, with high winds and perhaps accompanied by lightning. Being on a high point or tower during a lightning storm can unnerve the strongest person. If you wish to rent one of these places, come prepared by educating yourself and having the proper equipment and knowledge to use it.

These remote facilities have received a lot of publicity and hence are becoming more difficult to reserve. It is unlikely that you will be able to reserve the days you want with only a month or two's notice. Contact the appropriate Ranger District well in advance and you too may be rewarded with an indoor-outdoor experience.

There are many cabins and guard stations available to rent in our National Forests. In order to obtain a list of these facilities, contact the following regional National Forest headquarters and ask for the *Recreational Cabin and Lookout Directory:*

Region 1 – Montana and Northern Idaho
Northern Region
Federal Building
PO Box 7669
Missoula, MT 59807-7669
406-329-3511

Region 2 – Colorado, Wyoming, South Dakota
Rocky Mountain Region
740 Simms Street
PO Box 25127
Lakewood, CO 80225
303-275-5350

Region 3 – Arizona and New Mexico
Southwestern Region
Federal Building
517 Gold Ave, SW
Albuquerque, NM 87102
505-842-3292

Region 4 – Idaho, Nevada, Utah and Wyoming
Intermountain Region
Federal Building
324 25th Street
Ogden, UT 84401-2310
801-625-5352

Region 5 – California
Pacific Southwest Region
630 Sansome Street
San Francisco, CA 94111
415-705-2874

Region 6 – Oregon and Washington
Pacific Northwest Region
333 Southwest 1st Ave.
PO Box 3623
Portland, OR 97208
503-326-2971

ABOUT THE AUTHOR

David Calahan was born in Oregon in 1948 and except for two years in the Army, has spent most of his life there. Home is an isolated eighty-acre ranch in the Applegate Valley shared with his wife, fine artist and illustrator Barbara Kostal.

A professional firefighter for twenty years, he loves life, the outdoors, flying an ultralight, rafting, traveling, and riding a Harley Davidson motorcycle.

Inspiration for Snow Camp Lookout came as David and Barbara were entertained by other visitors' observations in the journal.

Book Ordering Information

Mail orders To: David Calahan
PO Box 1394
Jacksonville, OR 97530

Please send _____ copies of *Snow Camp Lookout* to the following:

Name _____
PLEASE PRINT

Address _____

City _____

State, Zip _____ _____

Phone (_____)_____

Book: $14.00 each, U.S. Funds (No State Sales Tax)

Postage and Handling:
$3.00 for the first book and 75 cents for each
additional book.

$4.00 Priority mail in U.S.A.

Payment:
☐ Check   ☐ Money Order   Total Enclosed $ _____

Gift to a Friend:

Name _____
PLEASE PRINT

Address _____

City _____

State, Zip _____ _____

Phone (_____) _____

For quantity discounts,
contact the author at the above address or
FAX (541) 899-7282.
Thank You